Praise for *Opportunity and Hope*

"Naomi Riley's book demonstrates what works for all our children—programs like Children's Scholarship Fund, which allow parents to choose schools that best serve their children's needs. At Trey Whitfield School, I've seen first-hand that when students get the right start, college can become a reality, not just a dream." —**A. B. Whitfield**, cofounder and COO of Trey Whitfield School, Brooklyn, NY

"*Opportunity and Hope* tells a beautiful story of the magic that can occur—and the lives that can be transformed—when children are given the opportunity to attend great schools. The key is that parents can choose which school is best for their children—a right that all wealthy parents have, but poor parents didn't until Children's Scholarship Fund came along. Read this book—and then join the fight to give all parents educational options for their children." —**Whitney Tilson**, managing partner, Kase Capital Management; education reform advocate

"Through the inspirational stories of ten students, Naomi Schaefer Riley makes a compelling case that all families deserve a say in their children's education." —**Matthew M. Chingos**, fellow, Brookings Institution, Brown Center on Education Policy

OPPORTUNITY AND HOPE

OPPORTUNITY AND HOPE

Transforming Children's Lives through Scholarships

Naomi Schaefer Riley

ROWMAN & LITTLEFIELD
Lanham • Boulder • New York • Toronto • Plymouth, UK

Published by Rowman & Littlefield
4501 Forbes Boulevard, Suite 200, Lanham, Maryland 20706
www.rowman.com

10 Thornbury Road, Plymouth PL6 7PP, United Kingdom

British Library Cataloguing in Publication Information Available

Library of Congress Cataloging-in-Publication Data

Riley, Naomi Schaefer.
Opportunity and hope : transforming children's lives through scholarship / Naomi Schaefer Riley.
pages cm
Includes bibliographical references and index.
ISBN 978-1-4422-2609-8 (cloth : alk. paper)—ISBN 978-1-4422-2610-4 (electronic) 1. Children's Scholarship Fund. 2. Children with social disabilities—Scholarships, fellowships, etc—United States—Case studies. 3. Children with social disabilities—Education—United States—Case studies. 4. Private schools—Economic aspects—United States—Case studies. 5. Social mobility—United States—Case studies. I. Title.
LC243.C47R55 2014
371.2'23—dc23
2014003616

Printed in the United States of America

CONTENTS

ACKNOWLEDGMENTS

It is difficult to imagine a more inspiring group of people to interview than the young men and women profiled in these pages. The recipients of these scholarships have been so forthcoming about the struggles and triumphs that they experienced on their journeys, and I cannot begin to thank them and their families for their openness and honesty.

The teachers and school administrators who supported these young scholars are too seldom recognized for their efforts. But I hope that the readers of this book will join me in realizing just how much their students—and all of us—owe to them. Without the teachers and administrators of these schools, we would not be welcoming such an impressive cohort of young adults into our colleges, our workplaces, and our communities.

I'd also like to thank the managers of these scholarship programs for arranging my visits and interviews. They are the ones out there on the front lines, connecting generous donors and high-quality schools with families in desperate need of better options for their children.

Finally, I'd like to recognize the vital support of Frank E. Baxter, the Bill and Susan Oberndorf Foundation, Michael Sall, and the William E. Simon Foundation. Your help with this project and your continued efforts to empower families to seek better educational opportunities are an inspiration.

INTRODUCTION

Every year, a glossy, ad-stuffed publication called *Westchester* magazine puts out a ranking of the public school systems in the northern suburbs of New York City. If you go to a dentist's or pediatrician's office in the ensuing months, chances are you'll see parents perusing the issue, looking for their town's schools and wondering why the kids in another town seem to have higher SAT scores or more Intel scholars or a greater number of admissions to Ivy League schools. The parents may not pick up and move their families as a result, but you can bet the school system was a factor in their decision to leave New York City and buy a house here in the first place. In fact, the best place to find a copy of *Westchester* magazine is in the office of a real estate agent. When parents spend their hard-earned money to move to one of the most expensive counties in the country, they want to know that there will be "excellent public schools" available for their kids.

Poke a little fun at them if you want, but these middle- and upper-class parents are doing what most parents do if they can afford it—choosing the best education they can find for their children, whether it's their neighborhood public school, a charter school, a private school or a religious school.

When it came time for the oldest of our three children to start kindergarten, my husband and I weighed all of our options carefully. We visited different schools, talked to teachers, principals, and other parents. We read everything we could get our hands on about the best ways for young children to learn. We still do.

Of course, like all parents, we are the first educators of our children. We teach them at home the skills we think they will need to succeed in an academic setting. We give them what we hope will be a moral compass to guide them in difficult situations. We set expectations of how we would like them to behave around other children and adults. Like all parents, we want a school that will support rather than undermine the education we have offered them. We expect a school that will turn the dreams we have for our children (and the ones they have for themselves) into realities.

But many parents have no choice about where to send their children to school. Because they cannot afford private school or a move to the suburbs, these mothers and fathers cannot do what they think is best for their families. Their hands are tied. As a parent, it breaks my heart.

American schools are not the engines of social mobility that they used to be. There are many reasons for this, and while we needn't give up thinking about long-term efforts to reform all schools, there are few easy solutions. What is critical to understand is that the situation is particularly challenging for African American and Latino children, among whom a majority of fourth graders struggle to read a simple children's book.[1] The gap widens the longer the child is in school. Black and Latino twelfth graders read and do math at the same level as white eighth graders.[2] And on average, close to half of all public high school students in urban areas, many of whom are minorities, drop out of high school.[3] (The most recent numbers for New York City show that only 55 percent of African American students and about 52.7 percent of Latino students graduated on time in 2012.)[4]

Yet there are signs of progress. Hundreds of thousands of children in urban areas across the country are graduating from high school, going to college, launching professional careers, and planting themselves firmly in the middle class—thanks to education alternatives that empower parents. From charter schools to publicly and privately funded scholarships to more public school choice, more and more children from low-income and minority families are getting the schools they choose and the education they deserve.

One of the leaders of bringing parents this choice is Children's Scholarship Fund (CSF). Launched in 1998 through the efforts of philanthropists Ted Forstmann and John Walton, CSF offered forty thousand low-income children across the country the chance to attend private schools for four years. From the outset, CSF has had bipartisan appeal—in fact, you might say it was more Democrat than Republican. At the 1999 ceremony announcing the awarding of the first scholarships, Ted Forstmann noted that as he and John Walton were putting together the board, he remembered saying to his partner, "'John, the way things are going with this board, you and I are going to end up being the only Republicans.' And John replied, 'Teddy, I think there's something I better tell you: I'm not a Republican either.'"

By the end of the application period in 1998, CSF had received scholarship requests from the parents of 1.25 million children from twenty thousand communities in all fifty states. This was an important moment for school choice since it evidenced the fact that low-income parents, just like the parents in Westchester, want the opportunity to make the best educational choices for their children.

The scholarships are only partial and the scholarship amounts are determined by the family's income and household size. The average CSF family in New York, for example, has an annual income of only $26,782, yet each family must contribute at least $500 a year toward their children's education, giving them a financial stake in the child's education and strengthening the family's role in the process. The great majority of CSF families are Latino or African American, but recipients also include immigrants from India, China, Poland, and many other countries. CSF serves a large number of single mothers and grandparents who are raising their grandchildren.

As of the 2013–2014 school year, CSF has provided scholarships worth more than $568 million, impacting the lives of more than 139,000 low-income children. Nationally, in 2013–2014, CSF funded scholarships for more than 27,650 low-income children in collaboration with its twenty-seven partner programs, which include the Denver, Charlotte, Newark, San Francisco, Omaha, New York, and Philadelphia programs featured in this book.

The stories of these children and their families are nothing less than inspirational.

The recurring themes I heard in the interviews I conducted were ones of improved academic outcomes, solid foundations for high school, college, and beyond, and a profound gratitude and desire to give back.

They are a testament to how empowering parents to make decisions about their children's education can change the trajectory of a child's life. And they are proof that given the right education, anyone can achieve the American dream. As Silas Farley, one of the alumni I interviewed, told me, "I've been incredibly blessed. I can't imagine being who I am apart from Children's Scholarship Fund because CSF put me in the settings where a whole village of nurturers trained me to be the person I am." Scholarships open the first doors of opportunity that keep opening to new doors of opportunity for the rest of a child's life.

Stories like the ones in this book are not just tales of individual accomplishment. When they reach a critical mass, these success stories hold the keys to raising up a whole community, to breaking the cycle of poverty, to increasing social mobility. If we can affect the life of one child, we can affect whole families and whole neighborhoods. When a child of immigrants learns to speak and read and write English well, when the child of unemployed or underemployed parents graduates from college, when a child who grows up living hand-to-mouth is able to save enough money to buy his own house, he will bring up the entire community. Together, these children will ensure that the next generation gets its shot at the middle class.

All of the scholarship recipients I interviewed made it a point to mention the ways they hope to pass on to others the good fortune that CSF has given them. As one young man told me, "That's my goal, to be extremely successful and just help people who came from the same situation as me. I would get a kid from public school and invest in his education. . . . If more people would get the opportunity I was given, the world would be a better place."

And there is plenty of evidence that education is the key component to this transformation. Paul Peterson of Harvard University and Eric Hanushek of the Hoover Institution found a strong connection between student achievement and economic prosperity. "Raising student test scores in this country up to the level in Canada would dramatically increase economic growth. We estimate that the additional growth dividend has a present value of $77 trillion over the next eighty years. This is equivalent to adding an average 20 percent to the paycheck of every worker for every year of work over this time period."[5] Imagine what that kind of boost would do for people in low-income neighborhoods!

There are many causes for hope. Thousands more parents are empowered to make quality choices for their children than in 1999 when CSF offered its first scholarships.

For example, some districts have become open to the idea of letting students in failing public schools choose a different neighborhood school or a charter school. In California, a "parent trigger" law has begun to allow parents with children in failing schools to transform their school into a charter school and choose a new direction for their children's education.

In 2012–2013, there were thirty-two publicly funded school choice programs (which allow parents to choose private schools) around the country, which included sixteen voucher programs, fourteen scholarship tax-credit programs, one education savings account program, and one individual tuition tax credit of significant size.[6] For the 2012–2013 school year, more than $960 million was dedicated to these programs, which have been enacted in sixteen different states and the District of Columbia.[7] Almost 250,000 students are participating in publicly funded school choice programs across the country, up from 12,000 children when CSF first launched.[8]

News of their success is spreading. In the 2011–2012 legislative session, thirty-five legislative chambers passed private school choice legislation in nineteen states.[9] But there are many battles on this important issue yet to be fought.

And there is every reason to continue promoting charter schools and other alternative public models. In the 2012–2013 school year there were 2.2 million kids in charter schools compared to less than 350,000 when CSF launched.[10] Still, the best ones hold lotteries each year and turn away many more kids than they accept.

Meanwhile there were 5.2 million students enrolled in private schools like the ones CSF students attend, 2 million in Catholic schools alone.[11] In principle, these schools have enough empty seats to accommodate the kids who are stuck in failing schools today. In fact, enrollment at these schools is dwindling because fewer and fewer parents in these neighborhoods can afford tuition and the schools themselves can only afford to subsidize so much.

The scale of the problem is far too large to be solved, in the short term, by private philanthropy alone. It is truly time for families to be empowered with the choice of where to send their kids to school. It is time for individuals and businesses who care about the future of their communities and the job-preparedness of their young people to direct their tax dollars to help families make this choice. It is time to let parents who most have the interests of their children at heart decide for themselves where they can receive the best education.

Offering parents a scholarship for their kids to attend a private school is something that works. There have been many studies showing higher high school graduation rates and improved test scores for scholarship recipients. A recent Brookings/Harvard study found that African American students in New York who won and used a scholarship to attend private school starting in kindergarten were 24 percent more likely to attend college than those who applied but didn't win a scholarship.[12] In a recent survey of its own alumni, CSF found that the vast majority (90 percent) plan to attend a four-year college. Of the cohort of CSF alumni in New York who graduated eighth grade in 2008, 98.5 percent reported that they graduated high school on time in 2012, and 92.5 percent went on to enroll in college. Overwhelmingly, their families said that their experience in private elementary school with CSF scholarships prepared the students for high school (95 percent agreed with this statement).

To understand what it means for parents to be able to choose the school that best matches their kids' needs, to be given the means to fulfill what they see as their deepest obligations to their families, it is necessary to hear their stories. In the chapters that follow, you will see not only the difficult circumstances which led many of these families to CSF but the hard work and the utter single-mindedness that made it possible for these parents to contribute to their children's education. You will see not only the hope that accompanied these children to their first day at a new school, the one their parents really wanted them to attend, but the realization of their children's dreams. Not only did they discover a love of learning once they were in the right environment, but they found teachers and counselors to help them get into college and eventually find a fulfilling career.

One young scholarship recipient in Florida told me she feels confident she will be able to do college-level work because her teachers have taught her how to read and study independently. They taught her how to ride, and then they "let go of the bicycle."

Even now, long after they have finished school, in some cases years into their professions, many of these young men and women describe coming back to their schools to seek out the advice and support of their teachers. Their parents, their first educators, put them on the right path. CSF allowed them to choose the schools that best matched their needs. Their teachers kept them focused and made them ready. But now it is the students themselves who are ready to make the next choices.

I

"NO ONE EVER TOLD ME I WAS DREAMING TOO BIG"

Recent Columbia University graduate Jason Tejada at the offices of Children's Scholarship Fund in New York City. *Courtesy of Children's Scholarship Fund.*

Jason Tejada is perfectly aware of how things could have turned out for him. Instead of working as an analyst in the Chief Investment Office of JPMorgan Chase, Jason could have become more like his cousin (a couple of years younger) who is into what Jason calls "the drug life." Up until around eighth grade, his cousin did all of his schoolwork and Jason says he "was close to a genius." But he attended a rough public school and the other kids mocked him for being a "nerd." So gradually but purposefully, his cousin changed to fit into his environment.

Jason, on the other hand, says he never encountered anything but respect from his classmates at the Incarnation School in Washington Heights in northern Manhattan, where he went from fifth through eighth grade. The other kids knew he was on the honor roll consistently, but his success made him, if anything, a leader among his peers.

One afternoon a few weeks before the end of his junior year in college, Jason and I return to Incarnation. The building is sandwiched among apartments and bodegas. You might not notice the school but for the fact that the block is barricaded on either end to allow students to enter and exit safely. The hallways are bright and each staircase landing is decorated with children's artwork. But the furnishings have not been updated in a long time.

Our interview is delayed by a few minutes because his former teachers are anxious to hear how Jason is doing. Finally an announcement is made over the staticky intercom system instructing them to please, *please*, let Jason return to the main office. Over six feet tall, he hurdles down the stairs and arrives dressed in dark pinstriped slacks and a light blue collared shirt that is open at the top. He has dark hair and a wisp of a mustache and some Gucci eyeglasses. A bit of the adolescent gawkiness remains, but he also has an easy smile and an air of confidence with strangers that some middle-aged men never develop.

Jason is sweating after making the rounds of this un-air-conditioned building on a warm May afternoon. Even though he hasn't gone away more than a few miles to college, he doesn't get back here often to visit. He is caught up in his adult life and his teachers say this is as it should be.

We stand for a minute chatting at the edge of the basketball court where Jason played in middle school. A teacher is setting up chairs and tables for a sports awards dinner to be held in a few hours. Our conversation is punctuated by the antiquated sound system that is being tested in advance of the event. Jason seems at home here, but a little reluctant to be the center of all this attention. His teachers see him as "all grown up" and one of Incarnation's many success stories (189 CSF Scholars attended Incarnation in the 2013–2014 school year), but Jason still looks up to them—figuratively, if not literally. They helped him overcome seemingly insurmountable obstacles to arrive where he has today. And he continues to seek their counsel when he is faced with a difficult decision.

The atmosphere at Incarnation improved the odds of Jason's success. But even going to a school in which everyone from the youngest students to the most senior administrators value academic performance hardly guarantees the kind of outcomes Jason has achieved. Throughout our conversation, Jason offers himself hypotheticals—what if I had gone to a different middle school? A different high school? Had a different family? Different teachers?—and then suggests it is impossible to imagine taking out any part of this equation.

Natural ability has no doubt played some role in Jason's success. And so, obviously, did Jason's parents. They came here from the Dominican Republic shortly before Jason was born. His father has since then worked long hours as a tailor and his mother helped out with the business too.

Jason's mother was determined that he and his two younger sisters would go to college. Luz Tejada wanted her children to aim high, but also to remember their values. "As parents, we wish the best for our children. I hope to see all three of them become professionals with careers."

She knew enough about their neighborhood in the Bronx and its schools to realize that unless she acted early, her dreams for her children would not become a reality. So she began trying to get Jason scholarships to private schools. The summer before fourth grade in 2000, Jason was awarded a grant from Children's Scholarship Fund. His mother wanted to use it toward sending Jason to a Catholic school since that was their own religious background, but the classes were already filled. So he spent a year at a Greek Orthodox school before landing at Incarnation in the fifth grade.

His parents did have to make a small contribution to Jason's tuition each year, but Children's Scholarship Fund covered 75 percent of his tuition for the next five years. CSF was the first among many organizations to help Jason and his younger sisters. Still, it was a struggle for Jason's family to come up with this money.

CSF New York

Jason received his scholarship from Children's Scholarship Fund New York (CSF New York), which served more than eight thousand children during the 2013–2014 school year. It is the largest CSF scholarship program and is run from CSF's national headquarters in Manhattan. Parents of CSF scholars choose from more than two hundred private and parochial schools in the five boroughs of New York City, and CSF New York also administers scholarships in several counties north of the city. More than twenty-four thousand children have used CSF New York scholarships since 1999. One hundred and eighty-nine CSF scholars attended Jason's alma mater, Incarnation School, in 2013–2014.

What does Jason remember about the public school he went to for the first few years of his life? There were the drug busts on the corner nearby. There were fights inside the school. But the biggest difference between that school and Incarnation, he says, is that the latter "felt like a family"—like school was a continuation of home. It was clear from the beginning that his parents and teachers were working together. His parents didn't say, "'Oh your teachers will do their job and we'll do ours,'" Jason explains. "It was the same vision."

The first month of fifth grade was hard to forget. It was September 2001. One morning Jason left his class to go to the bathroom and when he came back, everyone was praying silently with their hands folded on their desks. He asked one of his classmates what happened. She told him, "The Twin Towers fell down." The students didn't really understand. Few had any connection to the victims—many didn't even know what the Twin Towers were.

Jason remembers how his teachers tried to "shelter" him during this terrible time, but they also emphasized the importance of prayer in the face of difficulty. Their strength and compassion provided an important foundation for the rest of his education.

Incarnation was founded in 1910 to serve the growing immigrant population in the Bronx. It began as a small affair but by 1937, there were 1,400 students and the parish was three-quarters Irish. In the mid-twentieth century, the neighborhood saw an influx of Cubans, Dominicans, and families from Central and South America. The ethnic makeup may have changed but the school's mission remained the same.

Still, enrollment at the school started to decline—by the 1980s, there were about six hundred students. Now there are only half that many. While the church has kept tuition relatively low at less than $4,000 per student (a fifth of what New York City spends for each student), many parents simply cannot afford it. But for those who are lucky enough to attend, Incarnation has an enormous impact. Its mission is to concentrate on the "intellectual, moral, spiritual, aesthetic, social, and physical growth of each student . . . within the context of Catholic doctrine and tradition."

This kind of formation suited Jason well. He liked school, but it was not easy. His parents spoke only Spanish at home. And although Jason was fluent in English by the time he arrived at Incarnation, he says it was not his strong suit. He had to work hard at writing well. And he still remembers how his sixth grade teacher required three drafts of even the shortest assignments. It's a practice that has stayed with him even in college. "Sometimes you feel like you want to get it out of the way. It's a ten-page paper. It's done. I don't want to read it again." But he does.

"It was a good old-fashioned Catholic education without the ruler hits," Jason jokes. His teachers maintained consistent and complete control over classrooms with as many as forty students in them. Reading, writing, and math skills were drilled, but Jason insists that the repetition did not diminish his appetite for learning. He has fond memories in particular of a history class he took in sixth grade.

"The way she taught it," he says of the teacher, "and the way she engages that material—it has still stuck with me until this day." He remembers sitting in his dorm room during his sophomore year at Columbia trying to decide on his major. He picked economics first: "That's a major [you choose] because you want a job." And for kids who grow up poor, who are children of immigrants and the first people in their families to go to college like Jason, that's what college means—a stable income, a middle-class life.

But then Jason says he asked himself: "Am I really capitalizing on my college education? These are four years that you explore the world. And I started thinking about history and I've always been fascinated with the

Greeks and Egyptians." So fascinated that he decided on a second major in ancient history.

The subject has influenced not only his intellectual development but also his spiritual formation. When I ask Jason about the role of religion in his education, he says he remembers being taught Catholic doctrines, but that the tenets of the faith "were not imposed" on him. Students were required to do community service of various sorts. He tutored after school. He delivered turkeys to those in need on Thanksgiving. And his school did encourage participation in the church. He remembers warmly a Saturday night in eighth grade when all of his friends were altar servers at church. "There were fifty of us!"

To be honest, he tells me, he doesn't attend church much now, but he has been giving a lot of thought to his faith and its connection to his education. In a class on ancient Egyptian history, Jason describes reading about the Eighteenth Dynasty and the rule of King Akhenaten, who tried to encourage the Egyptian people to adopt a belief in a single godhead, an early attempt at abstract monotheism. Akhenaten did not ultimately succeed. But it's possible, according to some, that his legacy lived on. Jason describes to me Freud's hypothesis that Moses was a part of the cult of Akhenaten, and that is the origin of the Judeo-Christian belief system. Jason is skeptical of this theory, but he is utterly taken with tracing various theological strains from the ancient world to the modern one.

It's possible that the young man sitting across the table from me in a basement classroom at Incarnation is trying to impress me with the knowledge that he has gained in college. And he has. But his enthusiasm for the subject matter is obvious. He offers various tidbits of ancient history in trying to explain his own personal beliefs about the truth and origins of Catholicism.

Though he shies away from talking about it, Jason had to wrestle with some difficult, life-changing issues at a very young age. In the spring of his eighth-grade year, Jason was diagnosed with non-Hodgkin's lymphoma. "They told me it was a tumor and I remember I left the doctor's office and I punched a wall in the hospital. I was frustrated and my mom was crying and I just walked ahead . . . I was so mad."

But Jason didn't go home. He went right back to school. The day was over, but after-school activities were in progress. "The first person I saw was my eighth-grade teacher and I just started crying. I could not stop crying." Throughout his treatments, Jason continued to find comfort from the staff at Incarnation. He remembers being in the emergency room at 2:00 a.m. and his mother saying to him that he could stay home from school the following day. It was the first time the woman who was pushing him so hard had ever suggested such a thing. And he said, "No, I'm gonna go."

Jason's treatments continued throughout the summer after eighth grade and into the following year. He stopped playing basketball at Incarnation, but he wanted to participate in school as much as possible. His yearbook entry includes everything from student council and stage crew for the school play to after-school tutoring and the math club. His teachers and fellow students, he recalls, did their best not to treat him any differently. He finished Incarnation as the eighth-grade valedictorian.

His scholarship from CSF led to another scholarship to attend a Catholic high school. His teachers advised him to choose All Hallows, a prestigious all-boys institution in the Bronx. It has been designated as one of the top fifty high schools in the country and it is nothing if not

Jason's eighth grade graduation photo from 2005. *Courtesy of the Tejada family.*

rigorous. Most of his friends chose a different school and Jason was tempted to as well, but when he went to the All Hallows open house and realized all of the opportunities that would be available to him there, he didn't even think about another option.

Jason was receiving chemotherapy treatments when his ninth-grade year began. He attended the orientation and remembers carrying his backpack full of books from one classroom to another. Just walking up stairs he was getting winded. "I was so fatigued. I felt useless."

Within a couple of days he was back in the hospital with a fever of 105. He missed the first two weeks of school at All Hallows and the administration offered him the chance to withdraw or to try home-schooling. He refused. One morning he woke up in the hospital to find a tall stack of textbooks next to him and a list of assignments. In the next two years, Jason's cancer went into remission, and he began to regain his strength and energy.

He started getting involved in after-school activities at All Hallows little by little. First he joined the math club, then the TV and media club. He started to take advantage of the school's television studio, making documentaries in his spare time. First a comic documentary, then one on the centennial of All Hallows. Next he tried his hand at student council.

All the while, and perhaps a little under the radar, Jason was taking difficult courses and achieving a very high grade point average. He says the transition from middle school to high school was not a very difficult one. Incarnation had instilled in him a strong work ethic. He was ranked number one in his class during all of his years at All Hallows. It was there that he really began to understand more about the world he would soon be entering. He snagged a summer internship at Bloom-berg. He still marvels that he was being paid $14 an hour as a high school student. ("I don't even make that in my work-study job at Columbia!") He began to see the possibilities in his future.

When it came time to apply for college, Jason thought that his grades would give him a good chance at CUNY. He thought Baruch College might be a good fit since he was interested in business. He remembers an eye-opening meeting with his college counselor at All Hallows where he explained his plan. She took at a look at his transcript and suggested he expand his search. "What about Harvard, Cornell, and Columbia?" she asked. Jason was flabbergasted. "I didn't know too much about college. I mean, who was I going to ask? She told me I needed a reality check."

Achievement Gaps Leave Children Behind

By graduating from high school *and* an Ivy League college, Jason Tojada has beaten the odds for children (especially boys) growing up in low-income, inner-city neighborhoods like his own. Unfortunately, statistics show very different outcomes for most children growing up in his zip code.

- High school graduation can be predicted with reasonable accuracy by a child's reading skill at the end of third grade. A person who is not at least a modestly skilled reader by that time is unlikely to graduate from high school.
- More than half of Hispanic and African American fourth graders lack even basic reading skills.
- Racial achievement gaps continue to grow the longer a child is in school. Between fourth and twelfth grade, the gap grows 41 percent for Latino students and 22 percent for African American students.
- African American and Latino students trail their white and Asian peers in a variety of measures including NAEP standardized test scores, SAT scores, on-time high school graduation, college enrollment, and college graduation.
- On average, close to half of public high school students in urban areas become high school dropouts. The most recent numbers for New York City show that only 55 percent of African American students and about 52.7 percent of Latino students graduated on time in 2012.

Sources:
http://www.aecf.org/~/media/Pubs/Initiatives/KIDS%20COUNT/123/
    2010KCSpecReport/Special%20Report%20Executive%20Summary.pdf
http://www.mckinseyonsociety.com/downloads/reports/Education/detailed_
    achievement_gap_findings.pdf
http://schools.nyc.gov/Accountability/data/GraduationDropoutReports/default.htm

Jason eventually was accepted to Columbia, Cornell, Penn, Syracuse, NYU, and Fordham, among others. He was waitlisted at Harvard.

Jason knows he beat the odds. "You come to this country, you come from a low economic background and you're a minority. And there are a lot of things that play against you, unfortunately." You will more than likely live in a neighborhood with higher crime rates. You will not have easy access to a quality education. You will have a harder time finding a job. And you will probably experience discrimination.

His parents obviously made every effort to counteract some of these effects, getting Jason and his sisters into better schools, making sure they stayed out of trouble.

Part of Jason's success, though, was in not listening to the cultural messages that told him he wasn't going to make it. He believes racism exists, but he doesn't think it is as pervasive as some people think it is. "Everyone doesn't have the intention of 'let's suppress all the blacks and Latinos.' Yes there are people like that in the world, but I don't think that's everyone's intention. The system may be flawed, but I think there are ways to work around the system, and ways to change the system." Jason says that he has always been surrounded by adults telling him he could do more. No one at school or at home has ever told him he was "dreaming too big."

Jason's college decision ultimately came down to Columbia and NYU. At the latter, he was admitted to a program that would have provided him with a job upon graduating, but he had to pursue a business-related major. Jason wasn't ready to commit to that yet, so he chose Columbia. But, he smiles, "I can always be mayor or president."

In addition to JPMorgan and Bloomberg, Jason has also interned at Goldman Sachs. He now moves seamlessly in the rarified world of Ivy League schools and investment banks. His friends in college attended the top prep schools in the country and had been gearing their whole lives toward attending an Ivy League university. But Jason has caught up quickly.

If you want to see how far he's come, just check out the second grade classroom we visit at Incarnation. As part of their after-school program, they are studying banks. They are learning about things like how to pick an ATM password and how to prevent identity theft. It's a strange topic until you realize how many of their parents are probably immigrants who speak little English and are not familiar with the way things work here.

When the teacher finds out where Jason is interning this summer, she asks if he can help her arrange a field trip to visit their local bank branch. Jason explains that he is not working for the commercial part of Chase, but ultimately he relents and says he will try to help.

Looking at these kids, it is easy to see how remote the Twin Towers must have felt to Jason and his classmates all those years ago. They could spend their whole lives in this neighborhood—never entering the Financial District or any of the city's elite institutions. But one also sees in these children the potential for Jason's achievements. They are unfailingly polite but they are also eager to speak with adults they've never met before. They pepper Jason with questions about college—Where is your school? What do you study? How can we go there? And they ask me about being a writer—What kind of stories do I write? Did I go to college? The teacher encourages them to share their aspirations with us. They raise their hands impatiently, confident in the knowledge that no one has ever accused them of dreaming too big either.

They ask the teacher if they can show us a presentation they had prepared the week before. Jason and I watch as the children hold up poster board diagrams and talk to us about what they've learned. They are poised and articulate. And they don't want us to leave. We are their connection to the world outside of theirs, the one they want to be in, even if they don't entirely understand it right now.

Jason's two younger sisters have had a glimpse into this world, thanks to their brother's experience. They were both recipients of CSF scholarships as well. Joandalys attended St. Jean Baptiste High School after Incarnation. She is now a sophomore at Hofstra University. Jorvelyn is a junior at Notre Dame High School in Manhattan. Jason has helped them with their homework, with applications for scholarships, and with applications to college. He knows that they feel a lot of pressure to do as well as he has, but he wants them to be able to enjoy these opportunities too.

Throughout our conversation at the end of his junior year, Jason keeps referring to a kind of "crisis" he is going through. Now that he is twenty-two and now that he is facing his senior year in college, he has to decide what to do next. He's thinking of going to law school or business school eventually. He talks to his friends and his teachers about what to do next. They tell him, "It's fine to not know what you want to do. You have goals. You are on the right track." They tell him to "breathe." This is the first time in Jason's life where the next step for him isn't obvious. And he is clearly a little worried. As I make my way out of Incarnation's building, Jason goes back to his teachers and starts to describe how things are going. All these years later, he knows they will help him find the right path, and no doubt they are proud of him now as he begins his career at JPMorgan.

2

A FAMILY FINDS REFUGE

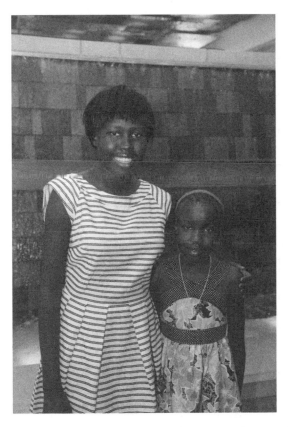

Nyawuor with her sister, Nyaduel, at a Children's Scholarship Fund of Omaha luncheon. *Courtesy of Children's Scholarship Fund of Omaha.*

There is such a concentration of Sudanese refugees in Omaha that in 2011, when it was time to set up polling places for a referendum on whether Southern Sudan should secede from the North, this Nebraska city of four hundred thousand was chosen as one of eight locations in the United States and forty-one worldwide for people to cast their ballots. In the 1990s, during the civil war in Sudan—a war that claimed some two million lives—Lutheran Family Services (under contract from the U.S. federal government) brought many Sudanese to the Midwest. They came from camps in Ethiopia, Chad, and Kenya. Many families literally had nothing but the clothes on their backs when they arrived.

Nyawuor Paljor's family went to California first in 1995 but then quickly moved to Omaha—employment prospects were better and the large Sudanese population (now close to fifteen thousand) was a big draw. Some of her extended family had already settled here. Her father began working at a company called First Data and then went back to school to get his associate's degree at a local community college.

Many of the Sudanese adults who came here were professionals in their home country, but since they did not know the language they were forced to start at the bottom and work their way back up—or hope their children could. The meatpacking plants in Omaha offer plenty of employment opportunities but the work is brutal and sometimes dangerous.

When they arrived in Omaha, Nyawuor's family moved into a government-assisted housing complex and she started attending the local public school. She says it was a "pretty negative environment." She recalls a lot of kids being sent each day to a detention room. There were security guards stationed at the doors of the school. It was crowded and Nyawuor didn't really get the academic attention she needed. She was reading at a lower level than everyone else—English wasn't her first language—but the teachers didn't seem to have the time or the inclination to get her up to speed.

Her cousins were attending All Saints Catholic School in Omaha, and Nyawuor's father felt this would be a good change. She tells me, "Living in the projects, we were always faced with a lot of violence from outside sources. My dad really wanted us to be reoriented in a safe education and not to get sidetracked by all these other things."

Her parents, needless to say, did not have the means to afford All Saints for Nyawuor and her siblings. They could barely afford food, clothing, and shelter for the family. That's when they applied for scholarships from Children's Scholarship Fund of Omaha. Since 2002 the fund has given scholarships to Nyawuor and her six younger siblings, the youngest of whom is in second grade now. In total, CSF has given almost a million dollars worth of scholarships to kids at All Saints in the past dozen years—$75,000 for the 2012–2013 school year alone. And many of the recipients are from the Sudanese community. Even with the consolidation of various parishes—All Saints serves three—the school still struggles to make ends meet and to help these lower-income families.

Children's Scholarship Fund of Omaha

Nyawuor Paljor and her siblings were recipients of scholarships from Children's Scholarship Fund of Omaha (CSF Omaha), which was established in 1999 when thirteen Omaha donors contributed $1 million to match a challenge grant from the national Children's Scholarship Fund. Since its founding, CSF Omaha has distributed scholarships worth more than $23 million to low-income children to attend eighty private and parochial schools in Omaha and northeast Nebraska.

As hard as it has been for the Catholic church to stretch its budget and welcome all of these strangers into their midst, Nyawuor will be forever grateful that CSF Omaha made it possible for her to attend All Saints School. New to the country, new to the language, and still healing from the past she left behind in Sudan, Nyawuor recalls how the teachers at All Saints nurtured her. A self-described introvert, Nyawuor describes how her second-grade teacher, Ms. Frasier, "really allowed me to become an individual. She helped me form opinions and ideas." Ms. Frasier made her want to "try harder in every subject." Her teacher "helped [her] understand why" they were studying the things they were.

Nyawuor's eighth-grade teacher also made a strong impact. "She didn't talk down to us. She would really encourage us." Faced with the decision of where to go to high school, Nyawuor recalls there being a lot of pressure. "She just helped us" get through that.

Today, Nyawuor is a model of composure. She is very quiet—a tall, slim young lady who is attending the University of Nebraska at Omaha. She hopes to earn a master's degree in social work after she graduates. Right now she juggles her schoolwork, a job of at least twenty hours a week at the local supermarket, and taking care of her six younger siblings.

Nyawuor's mother passed away during her freshman year of high school. The family then moved in with her uncle. Her father, meanwhile, has had trouble finding work locally so he has gone to Alaska for three months to work on fishing boats. Most of the time, the family cannot even reach him. He calls home by pay phone as often as he can. Two of Nyawuor's siblings were sent back to Sudan briefly to live with relatives because her father couldn't support and supervise everyone here.

I meet Nyawuor in the basement of All Saints, where the cafeteria is located. The building is old and could clearly use some new tables and chairs and another coat of paint. But these are not the priorities. It is located in an older section of town, a short drive from the business district, but some of the buildings nearby are abandoned. The teachers try to make up for these deficiencies by ensuring that the children have other opportunities beyond the classroom. The classes make regular trips to the local art museum and since the school has its own bus it can take the kids on relatively frequent field trips elsewhere.

Unlike many of the other young men and women I interviewed who come back to their schools once a year to visit teachers or attend a basketball game, Nyawuor is here as often as once a week to attend a school function or meet with one of her siblings' teachers.

Jennifer Nymann, Nyawuor's third-grade teacher, calls her a "gentle spirit." Nymann, who has one of Nyawuor's younger brothers in class this year, says "she has taken on the role of the mom in the family." Nymann reports, "She even signs his reading folder," acknowledging that he has done his work.

Nymann is "amazed" at what her former student has accomplished. "Here she is in college and trying to make her own way, but she is still so caring and loving to her brothers and sisters." It's not just the parental obligations. Nyawuor makes it a point to attend even optional events like a school movie night, determined that her siblings do not feel left out because they do not have a mother or father present.

Part of Nyawuor's strength seems to come from the Catholic religion. When she thinks about her teachers at All Saints, she says, "I think they wanted us to build on our faith. They wanted us to make something of ourselves," both in terms of their education and their spiritual life. She felt her faith was "reenergized" at All Saints. They had Mass three times a week and she says that receiving the sacraments had a major impact on her formation.

After All Saints, she chose Mercy High School, an all-girls Catholic school. While some of the girls attending had come from wealthier schools and better neighborhoods, Nyawuor felt that All Saints really prepared her. "The teachers helped me realize the importance of education and understand that I had to try harder."

By the time she got to high school, Nyawuor was reading at grade level. Because All Saints has welcomed so many Sudanese students, their teachers have become adept at teaching English as a second language and bringing their charges up to speed. According to All Saints principal Marlan Burki, about two-thirds of the students there do not speak English fluently. Even those who can speak it well enough "find reading more difficult." "Writing," he says, "is the hardest."

Private Schools, Public Citizens

As children of Sudanese immigrants, Nyawuor and her siblings relied heavily on their school to learn about American culture, history, and values. Fortunately, research finds that private schools such as All Saints, where Nyawuor completed elementary school, do a good job of preparing students for their future role as citizens, including making it more likely they will vote. A study by Notre Dame's David Campbell found higher levels of community service, civic engagement, political knowledge, and political tolerance among private school students, with Catholic school students showing the highest levels of voluntarism and political tolerance.

Sources:
http://www.law2.byu.edu/lawreview/archives/2008/2/92CAMPBELL.pdf
http://educationnext.org/civics-exam/

From an academic perspective, though, the commitment of schools like All Saints to rapidly bring the language skills of immigrant children up to grade level is another important factor in making these newcomers feel welcome here and preparing them for high school and college. While many schools might put these students into segregated ESL classes or simply let them fall behind, All Saints has determined that it is much more important to get these students used to being in regular classes.

Because there are so many kids who have special language needs, the school cannot put more than twenty children in a class. This places a serious strain on the budget. Whereas most states allot more money to children in public schools with special needs, Catholic schools cannot charge more for these students. Private schools must make do with whatever tuition they collect, regardless of how much help a student might need.

Burki says the teachers find an immense sense of satisfaction in their work. A teacher for many years before arriving at his position, Burki says: "The neat thing for us is that we get to see a tremendous amount of growth. A fifth grader who was reading at a first grade level when he came in this year is now reading at grade level."

He insists, "These kids are very intelligent, but they just don't know the language yet." Nyawuor says that the intensive work she did at All Saints in language meant that in high school she was able to complete the long reading assignments and write the research papers as well.

For Nyawuor, the expectation at All Saints, at Mercy, and at home was always the same: She would go to a four-year college. "It wasn't really something that we would negotiate," she says quietly.

In addition to the courses preparing her for a social work degree, Nyawuor also took a number of English and political science courses, and she considered majoring in the latter. She has always liked history and never minded "memorizing information." She says she loves how "it's an ongoing story, so everything connects."

With a life that began on one side of the world and now continues on the other, with a family that has been torn by tragedy but that is slowly working its way back together, it is easy to see why Nyawuor likes this idea of an ongoing story where everything connects.

She has settled on social work as a profession. More specifically, she hopes to work with children in foster care. It is hard to imagine how someone like Nyawuor, who has lived through so much and who devotes so much of her time to others, can have it in her to give back even more. But she tells me, "I think that because I was faced with different events in my life, I can help people who are faced with similar things."

She says that her father's hard work as the sole parent to seven children has "really motivated" her. "We lived in assisted housing a lot of my life and I kind of just understand people, I can relate to where people are right now and I just want to help them get out of it."

Nyawuor says that it was hard at first to balance going to work, going to school, and her responsibilities at home. But she says that she learned at All Saints, "What is most important is education and everything else circled around that." All Saints has allowed Nyawuor and her siblings to make sure that education is always the priority. Like many schools discussed in this book, All Saints opens early and stays open later for parents whose work schedules cannot accommodate school hours. Nyawuor's siblings are among the first in the building at 6:30 a.m. (All Saints gives them breakfast) and they are driven home in the afternoon on a bus that is also paid for by the school. None of these experiences would be possible without scholarships from CSF Omaha.

In a few years, with any luck and a lot of work from the children and their teachers at All Saints, Nyawuor's siblings will also follow her to college and into stable lives in middle-class America. Seeing this process unfold has been extremely rewarding for the teachers who have been present for the great Sudanese migration.

Jennifer Nymann describes how her own daughters, who attended All Saints with many of these refugee children, would occasionally go to visit their friends in the more depressed areas of town. First, Nymann recalls driving her daughters to the projects. Then a few years later, more of the Sudanese lived in small apartments in South Omaha. And then finally, some of them moved into single-family homes in better neighborhoods. The children, according to Nymann, were so proud to show her that their families had their own houses. Nymann and Burki both told me that it was deeply moving for them to watch, over the course of a little more than a decade, the Sudanese community go from strangers in their community to people who have put down roots here, who have been able to climb the economic and social ladder in their city.

This is what Catholic schools have done for the past century and a half. They have moved immigrant groups—one after another—into mainstream America. It began with the Polish, the Irish, and the Italians, but it later came to include waves of newcomers from Mexico, the Caribbean, South America, Africa, and Asia.

It seems ironic now that when Catholic schools were first formed in the nineteenth century, many observers worried that they would act as separatist influences, allowing immigrant groups to keep too much of their ethnic and religious loyalties and never helping them fit in here. Nativist groups in America suggested that Catholics schools would reinforce "dual loyalties" among citizens.

In response, groups like the Know Nothing Party supported an expansion of the public schools and restrictions on the extent to which Catholic students could be accommodated at those institutions. For instance, the Know Nothings pushed for allowing only Protestant teachers and for using only the King James Version of the Bible in the classroom.

The nativists also supported laws to prevent religious schools from receiving any taxpayer dollars. These so-called Blaine Amendments, named for Maine senator James G. Blaine who wanted the rule to be added to the federal constitution, remain on the books in many states today.

Contrary to the concerns of these early critics, private schools have hardly served as a vehicle for the self-segregation of immigrants. Patrick Wolf of the University of Arkansas recently conducted a review of the research on tolerance and civic engagement of students at public versus private schools. He identified twenty-one studies of the effect that public and private schooling have on political tolerance. (Tolerance is typically identified by asking students to identify their least favorite group and then asking if they would allow them to speak freely.)

Of the studies, some of which were conducted by researchers at Harvard, Notre Dame, and the University of Chicago, only one—focusing on non-Catholic religious schools—found that public school students are more tolerant. Eleven studies found that private school students are significantly more likely to be tolerant, and nine found no difference.[1]

One of the studies, conducted using interviews with students in Washington, DC, allowed researchers to control for a variety of other factors by comparing students who were picked to be a part of the DC voucher program and those who applied but were not chosen by the lottery. As Wolf wrote in the journal *Education Next*: "Nearly one-half of the students who switched to a private school said they would permit a member of their disliked group to live in their neighborhood, compared with just over one-quarter of the students in the public school control group."

Whether it is their messages about respecting the dignity of others or some other factor, it seems clear that private schools do a good job of conveying our national values regarding tolerance and the importance of assimilation to children from a variety of backgrounds.

For Nyawuor, her siblings, and the other members of the Sudanese refugee community, the opportunity to attend a Catholic school with a CSF scholarship was an important part of easing their transition into American life. Both academically (helping them learn English quickly) and culturally (teaching tolerance for others), All Saints may have been the most important institution for the community. Lutheran Family Services may have brought the refugees here, but the schools that Nyawuor's family was given access to with scholarship assistance have been a constant source of support over the fifteen years that they have lived in Omaha. It is the schools that have allowed Nyawuor and her brothers and sisters to feel like they belong in America and CSF is part of that story.

3

CALLED TO DANCE

Silas Farley performing in George Balanchine's *Cortège Hongrois* **during the School of American Ballet's Workshop Performances in 2012.** *Choreography George Balanchine © The George Balanchine Trust. Photo © Paul Kolnik.*

In March of 2013, the *Wall Street Journal* reported on the School of American Ballet's annual Winter Ball. The attendees were some of the city's most prominent financiers, actors, philanthropists and designers—including "ballet legend Mikhail Baryshnikov, designer Carolina Herrera and David Koch." But then the article went on to say, "the biggest star of the night was arguably SAB student, Silas Farley, 18 years old, who choreographed the evening's performance."[1]

So how did Farley, a boy from a mixed-race, working-class family of seven kids in North Carolina, receive what one critic called the "rare honor" of being asked to choreograph for the Winter Ball? It's a long story, but at the center of it are Silas's parents, his teachers, and Children's Scholarship Fund.

It was not easy to get a meeting with Silas—his rehearsal schedule keeps him very busy—but when I sit down with him in the Manhattan offices of CSF, the tall, lanky young man with high cheekbones is deeply gracious. He is also, not surprisingly, deeply graceful. Silas is casually dressed in jeans and a polo shirt and a fleece, but he arranges himself carefully in his seat, from his long fingers to his long feet.

He tells me how his family moved from Virginia Beach to Charlotte, North Carolina, when he was very young. Unfortunately, the only home they could afford on his father's salary as a musician was near what he calls "the least funded, lowest performing" schools. His mother decided to homeschool the children. In the morning, before his father left for work, he would do math drills with the kids, and then his mother would take over, teaching them literature and other subjects. "It was a labor of love, totally, from the two of them," says Silas.

For eleven years, it seemed, love was enough. But when Silas's older siblings got to high school, things became more "complicated." "How are we going to do chemistry in the kitchen?" his mother wondered aloud. They tried working with other homeschooling parents splitting up the subjects so that kids would get instruction from the adults with the most expertise. But with seven children, it was logistically very difficult.

Silas's parents decided to ask Children's Scholarship Fund–Charlotte for help. Falinda Farley had been told about CSF by a pastor she met in her church parking lot. He insisted that she fill out an application. The Farleys were put on a wait list for three and a half years. One day, Falinda recalls, a thick manila envelope arrived in the mail. She thought it was another notice that they had been passed over again. When she realized that her family had been accepted, she screamed so loudly that "my husband, who was shaving, nearly cut his neck off." The letter, she recalls gratefully, said "Welcome to the CSF family."

CSF Charlotte

Founded in 1999 by Julian H. Robertson Jr., Children's Scholarship Fund–Charlotte (CSF-C) has invested more than $7.2 million in scholarships benefitting more than 5,150 local schoolchildren, including Silas Farley and his siblings. CSF-C receives matching funds from the national Children's Scholarship Fund. Almost four hundred Charlotte area children were using CSF-C scholarships in 2013–2014.

By the time the scholarship became available, Falinda says, home-schooling simply wasn't feasible anymore. "I just wanted to be their cheerleader," not their school teacher. If they hadn't received the scholarship, she says, "I don't know what we would have done." Silas recalls, "It was just at the moment where they felt they had come to their wits' end" that his parents learned the kids had been chosen to receive scholarships. "It was an enormous blessing."

At the time, the family was attending the Resurrection Lutheran Church and it was a short drive from the Farley home, so Silas started out at the school there and stayed through third grade. "Mom and Dad wanted us to be in an environment where we would not only be academically challenged and nurtured but also spiritually challenged and nurtured so that the whole person would be cultivated." From Resurrection, Silas went on to two more faith-based schools—Trinity Episcopalian and Charlotte Christian.

"The same kind of hope our parents had for us, they saw reflected in the missions at the particular schools they sent us to," says Silas. All three institutions were "trying to cultivate the whole child." Silas thinks back to Resurrection Christian often. When he is on his way to ballet class on Friday mornings near Lincoln Center in Manhattan, he thinks of Friday morning chapel in school. "It was the community time, it was the whole school." He also remembers one of his earliest performances there—acting in a class performance of the Prodigal Son, set in the Wild West.

Silas's mother actually worked at Resurrection as an assistant teacher. She bartered her services for discounts on her children's tuition. Private school was clearly a sacrifice for the Farley family but they were willing to throw whatever time and money they had into ensuring their children had the best education available.

And the children's talents were to be nurtured as much as possible too. Silas had four very athletic older brothers. One of them, Matthias, is a safety for the University of Notre Dame's football team. He has other siblings who have attended Princeton and Vassar. But Silas's mother noticed early on that her youngest child didn't seem particularly interested in any of the traditional options—baseball, football, or basketball—that his siblings had excelled in. Though Silas was clearly athletically inclined too, he preferred to sing and dance and act. One of the clear advantages to giving parents the choice of where to send their kids to school is that they probably understand best their children's interests as well as their strengths and weaknesses. Even for children in the same family, different school environments may be better.

She mentioned her son's interests to a woman who attended their church. That woman in turn put the Farleys in touch with a dance school called the King David Christian Conservatory. Silas went for a kind of audition, but his mother told the director that they couldn't afford the tuition. He offered to train Silas at a rate of $25 a month. "We'll take it out of the grocery money," she told him. "Whatever we have to do." Eventually Silas was paying nothing for his dance instruction because his father offered to teach the director's son how to play the drums.

Silas remembers vividly the first time he saw a ballet. There was a company that came to his church from Mississippi, the Ballet Magnificat. It was a Christian ballet company and Silas says he was "struck by the power of the male dancers." It wasn't "flitting around, but it also wasn't football. It was elegance. It was power and poetry wedded together."

But getting from a small Christian dance school in North Carolina to where he is today involved a lot of hard work, some funny coincidences, and some real "blessings," he tells me. While Silas was studying at King David, his mother happened to win a prize at a Christmas show, which

had to be picked up at the local public television station. It was there
she ran into a videographer for the North Carolina Dance Theatre, the
most prestigious dance school in Charlotte. The two got to chatting
about her son, and the videographer went back to the ballet company
and asked if Silas could get an audition.

Silas was accepted and trained with the North Carolina Dance Theatre from the time he was nine until he was fourteen. And that prepared
him to come to New York.

During those middle school years, Silas says his teachers were nothing but supportive of his dance aspirations. They even helped him to
develop his understanding of ballet. He recalls that his fifth-grade
teachers at Trinity encouraged students to read the books that interested them. Silas read dance biographies the whole year. "I wanted to
soak it all up and I was encouraged to do that in an academic setting,"
he recalls gratefully.

Falinda Farley says that allowing kids to pursue their own interests
through their reading was something she had done when she was homeschooling. Finding this same practice in a school confirmed for her that
she and her husband had made the right decision. "We weren't at odds
with the core of what school was teaching. It really was an extension of
our family and our Christian faith," she says.

Silas recalls one component of his reading program in fifth grade was
the "reading letter." At the end of each week, he would write a letter to
his teacher talking about the reading that he had done that week and
what he had learned from it. The teacher, in turn, would write back to
each student on Monday. "I look back on that and it was an incredible
amount of work for the teacher." He has recently reread some of those
letters. The kinds of questions they were asking him were provocative
and insightful.

Rather than wondering why Silas was reading only about dance, his
teachers would ask, "What have you learned about your art from this
book?" "What does the dancer's choice regarding their career mean for
you?" "How did this girl deal with being at a major company at that
young of an age?"

It wasn't only that Silas was learning about dance. He threw himself
into the study of literature and history. Silas and his classmates at Trinity Christian did a serious study of Shakespeare in fifth grade. Not only
did they practice reciting passages aloud, but the study was weaved into

other subjects as well. They learned what mathematic and scientific discoveries coincided with Shakespeare's life. They learned about Elizabethan history. Looking back, Silas says he was impressed that the school tried to tackle Shakespeare when the kids were so young. "It was presented to us at an age where your mind is still opening. You haven't had time to hear people say, 'Oh, Shakespeare's hard' or 'Oh, Shakespeare's boring.'"

Now that Silas is no longer in school, he is back to reading what most interests him. "Now and in fifth grade are probably the two times I've felt most free to explore in my reading."

His fifth grade year culminated in a production of *Romeo and Juliet*. Silas played Friar Laurence and still remembers the thrill of delivering those soliloquies. But he was also given the opportunity to choreograph the masquerade ball in the play. He gave his fellow fifth graders some "pretty difficult steps and rehearsed them very meticulously. I made them do lifts!" he adds, noting that he wished he had a videotape of the event.

His classmates, he assures me, were always very supportive of his pursuits too. Maybe it was because his older brother was a star football player, but his classmates never gave him a hard time about being a boy doing ballet. However, it also says something about the schools he attended that his fellow students had so much respect for each other.

Silas's teachers were wholly supportive of his extracurricular endeavors. It wasn't uncommon for them to attend his dance performances— "to cheer me on," he remembers. His teachers never compared Silas to his classmates and he admires the way they could meet every student "where they were." He had a hard time when he was younger understanding why his friends didn't have the same kind of intensity of purpose that he did. "When I was younger, there was a little part of me that wanted to say to people, 'Come on, find something. Focus. Let's get to work.'"

Looking back, he realizes it's not every kid who knows what he wants to do with his life at age nine. "It's such a blessing," he tells me. But he's never looked down on people who haven't had that kind of goal. "I know it's only by God's gift to me that I can dance and by His grace that He's given me the opportunities to dance." He says he only hopes that others will be able to find "their particular calling in life."

Silas strove for excellence in all of his academics, though he acknowledges that math and science weren't his best subjects. His schooling, particularly at Charlotte Christian, was conducted at the highest levels in all subjects. When it came time for him to go to New York, there was no question about his preparedness. Indeed, when he began at the Professional Children's School in Manhattan, he skipped the eighth grade and started in the ninth.

The school admits kids who are Broadway actors, dancers, musicians, and athletes who are already working at a professional level. Silas says it's a "very cool environment. There's no real competition because people . . . are already so distinguished in what they're doing outside of school." That being said, Silas is often in awe of his fellow students. "You were sitting around doing algebra" with kids who were in movies or on Broadway. He remembers walking down Fifth Avenue and seeing a giant picture of one of his friends from school, a model, in one of the store windows.

Being able to come to New York by himself for high school, to go to school and dance while his parents remained in North Carolina, was not really a big hurdle for Silas. He credits his parents and teachers for giving him the kind of spiritual foundation he needed in order to exercise that independence. "I felt so equipped," he says. "What our mom and dad trained us in, my own personal faith and my own understanding of the Bible, I felt like I was in a strong enough place that I could go into New York City and feel perfectly comfortable."

Though much of Silas's background was in a Christian world, he says that his family, his teachers, and his church community gave him the confidence to operate in a secular one. "We were raised to know that Jesus taught that you're supposed to love the people around you. That doesn't mean you have any shame for believing what you believe. It's just about embracing the people around you because if you ever want to see anybody change, you've got to meet them where they are."

As Silas tells the story of how he ended up at the School of American Ballet, all of the twists and turns along the way, he mentions the name (first and last) of every person who helped him through this process. If he can't recall one for a moment, he will not go on with his thought until he remembers it. "There were complicated wonderful stories at every juncture of my family's life." He says that he has "been given so much. It's incumbent upon me to make good on that investment."

"I've been incredibly blessed," he tells me. "I can't imagine being who I am apart from Children's Scholarship Fund because CSF put me in the settings where a whole village of nurturers trained me to be the person I am." Whenever he goes back to Charlotte, he makes it a point to visit his teachers and thank them "because I would not be where I am without them."

Silas's passion for dancing was clear from early on. He says that starting in first grade, it was like he had "two full-time jobs." One was going to school and the other was dancing. People often ask him about the sacrifices he had to make in order to devote so much time to dancing—birthday parties he missed or just having fun with other kids. But he says, "I never thought of it as a list of prohibitions. I knew when I was seven years old that I wanted to be a professional dancer. I knew from the time I was nine years old that I wanted to dance with the New York City Ballet. That was always my goal and I cared about it more

Silas Farley with parents, Mark and Falinda Farley, shortly after his graduation from Professional Children's School in 2012. *Courtesy of Children's Scholarship Fund.*

than anything else. It was what I loved." Silas says that he hasn't slept much in the past thirteen years but "it was all worth it."

He says that he wanted to "max out on every aspect of life." He received all As in school. His philosophy on these matters sounds like it comes from someone twenty years older: "More of life is spent in the getting there than in the actual result so to the degree that you can enjoy doing homework and stuff like that," it will be better for you. Silas didn't feel as though academics and dance were competing for his attention either. Both his school and his dance contributed to his "focus and perseverance."

But now Silas has been forced to make a choice. He finished high school last year and was admitted to Harvard University. He decided to defer his admission a year to give himself more time to dance. Now he is completing a kind of one-year probation, an apprenticeship, before he can become a regular member of the New York City Ballet. If the attention he is getting from the media and from Peter Martins, the ballet master in chief, is any indication, Silas is a shoe-in for a permanent spot with the corps de ballet. In addition to the Winter Ball, Silas has also planned and hosted the New York City Ballet children's seminar with members of the orchestra on stage. He offered a whole program on "Sleeping Beauty," with members of the company dancing various parts. Prior to Silas's arrival this had only been done by retired masters or principals in the company.

"I've been incredibly blessed. I can't imagine being who I am apart from Children's Scholarship Fund, because CSF put me in the settings where a whole village of nurturers trained me to be the person I am."

He couldn't defer Harvard for another year, however, while he waited to find out for sure whether he had earned a permanent spot. He had to either say yes to Harvard or to the chance of the New York City Ballet. He chose the latter. "My love of dance has always been total. It has not just been focused on being a good dancer. I knew I wanted to become a great teacher and a great choreographer and a ballet master." Even if he only has fifteen years or so of actual dancing ahead of him, those other skills are what he intends to work on for the rest of his life.

Homeschooling in the United States

Before Silas Farley used a CSF-Charlotte scholarship to attend private school, he and his siblings were homeschooled by their parents, something that's becoming increasingly common.

- According to the U.S. Census Bureau, more than 1.5 million children in the United States are being homeschooled (homeschooling groups put the number closer to 2 million), and homeschooling numbers have almost doubled since the late 1990s.
- Many factors—including religion, dissatisfaction with academics at local schools, safety concerns, family lifestyle/travel, and special needs, among others—influence a family's decision to take on the full-time education of their children.
- Regulations for homeschoolers vary by state, with some states requiring parents to submit a curriculum and portfolios of their children's work, while other states have minimal requirements.
- A 2003 survey of adults who had been homeschooled found that 92 percent believed homeschooling was advantageous to them as an adult and 95 percent were glad they had been homeschooled.
- Homeschooling has been legal in all fifty states since 1993.

Sources:
http://www.edweek.org/ew/issues/home-schooling/
http://nces.ed.gov/pubs2009/2009030.pdf

Silas may at some point take classes at Columbia University or another college in New York City and slowly work toward a degree. It's hard to fit too many other things into the schedule of a professional dancer. They take classes with the company each morning. They can be called to rehearse any time between noon and 7:00 p.m. every day. And during the season, they perform seven times a week.

Silas says he wants to "stay in the ballet world my whole life" rather than leave at some point to get a degree and pursue a different career. Still, he plans to bring the "curiosity and inquisitiveness" he has always had in his academic pursuits to his ballet. "I'm learning more by doing, by learning the ballets, by meeting the teachers, getting to know these incredible artists, but also reading a lot."

Silas is not a typical eighteen-year-old—not by a long shot. And no matter where he went to school, he probably would have found a way to shine. When you ask him what his life would have been like without the scholarships he received to attend private school, he is not sure how to answer. "I really can't even imagine." On the one hand, he says, "I know my parents. If something hadn't come through, they would have hunkered down and finished homeschooling all of us and I'm sure we would have all turned out well because we have pretty extraordinary parents. And that would just be a testament to their incredible sacrificial love and perseverance in spite of all obstacles."

Still, Silas says, nothing would have been equal to those years he had at Resurrection, Trinity, and Charlotte Christian. "The way that each of those schools was situated in my growth as a person" could not be replicated. The combination of the spiritual and academic strength that each of them instilled in him was vital to his success. Silas believes it was somehow "divinely orchestrated how each piece built off of the next so that I would be ready to come here at fourteen."

He thinks about how his teachers complemented his parents in the way he was brought up. "The only reason I am the person that I am is because of what mom and dad taught me . . . this unshakable center of me. And then the training I got in those academic settings. It was all so inextricably woven together to make me who I am. I can't really imagine who I'd be without those links of all those nurturers along the way." While we often talk about school officials acting in loco parentis, we mean it in a strictly legal sense. The teachers in Silas's life seemed to have been teaching Silas in the same way they would have if they were his parents. His teachers did not subvert the role of his mother and father, rather they became part of Silas's extended family.

And now Silas is taking on that role himself. In the fall, Peter Martins named Silas one of two students at the School of American Ballet to teach courses there. Martins's goal was to "pump new blood" into the school, as the *New York Times* put it. "When people decide to teach when they retire, it's too late," Martins said in an interview. "The obvious reason is, why? Do you want to have a paycheck? You can't be a teacher for that reason."

When Silas talks about his teachers, it is clear that he has a deep appreciation for what they have done. "The whole idea of ballet is that it could be passed down from person to person. It can't be simulated. You can't learn it from a video. Someone has to lay down their life and come into a studio and teach you patiently every day for years so you get to the level of mastery to actually be a dancer." For Silas, all of their work has clearly paid off.

POSTSCRIPT

Silas found out in July 2013 that he was accepted as a full member of the New York City Ballet. He wrote an e-mail to CSF saying:

> I received my corps de ballet contract yesterday morning. I am offi-
> cially a member of the New York City Ballet!!!!!! This is the dream
> I've had since I was 9 years old. Thank you for your prayers, guid-
> ance, and encouragement that have helped me get to this moment.

4

WHAT WOULD YOU DO IF YOU COULDN'T FAIL?

Cathiana Vital with Sister Patricia Hogan, principal, at Our Lady Help of Christians School in East Orange, NJ. *Courtesy of Children's Scholarship Fund.*

Doctor or lawyer: For as long as she can remember, those were the two choices that Cathiana Vital's parents would give her when they talked about her future profession. But it was clear by seventh grade that Cathiana planned to chart her own path. She excelled in math and art, and by the time she was a senior in high school, she had set her sights on a career in architecture.

Her parents were Haitian immigrants—they came here just before her older sister was born in 1980—and did not entirely understand what Cathiana was thinking with this architecture thing, she tells me. When she went to college and changed her mind—this time with a view to becoming a forensic accountant—they were even more baffled. But here she is, two years out of college, with a BS in accounting and marketing and an MS in information management from Syracuse University, and a full-time position at PricewaterhouseCoopers.

We meet early one Thursday morning at Our Lady Help of Christians in East Orange, New Jersey. The surrounding neighborhood seems surprisingly free of traffic at rush hour. The local Dunkin Donuts is crowded but most businesses around here are not booming. Cathiana lives nearby in Newark with her parents who still belong to this parish and come to church every Sunday. "I was baptized here. I had my First Communion here. I'm probably going to get married here," says Cathiana, laughing.

But Cathiana's family is among the few to hang on. With three hundred or so students, Our Lady Help of Christians is less than half the size it was when Cathiana attended. (More than fifty of the school's students were using scholarships from CSF's partner program, the Scholarship Fund for Inner-City Children, in 2013–2014.) Those families who have been able financially to leave the area have done so. Those who have stayed have been hit hard by the recession. Some cannot afford the school's tuition, and they have tried alternatives like a new charter school nearby. Many are simply stuck in the city's underperforming and often dangerous public schools, which is bad news for the next generation of children in this neighborhood.

Cathiana's mother was a nursing assistant and her father drives a taxi. They could not afford very much in the way of tuition. Cathiana doesn't remember the exact amount of her scholarship from the Scholarship Fund for Inner-City Children, but she knows that her parents paid so little that they could give Cathiana the amount they owed in tuition each month in cash and she could deliver it to the school office.

Her parents pushed her to work hard in school, but it was the school itself and the teachers at Our Lady Help of Christians that opened Cathiana's eyes to the spectrum of possibilities before her. They nurtured her love of drawing and her love of math. They encouraged her not only to apply to college, but to leave home for it. They gave her information about scholarships and helped with the applications.

Scholarship Fund for Inner-City Children (NJ)

The Scholarship Fund for Inner-City Children (SFIC), which funded Cathiana's scholarship to Our Lady of Help of Christians School, became a Children's Scholarship Fund partner program in 1998. In addition to the SFIC General Scholarship Program and a donor-designated scholarship program, which are funded independently, SFIC receives matching funds from CSF National to award scholarships to approximately four hundred children like Cathiana who attend private schools of all types in Newark, Elizabeth, and Jersey City, New Jersey.

Cathiana remembers her seventh-grade teacher, Ms. Morillo, with particular fondness. "I just learned so much academically and spiritually in her class. That was the first time I really loved math because of the way she taught it. There was a passion behind it." In one art class, Ms. Morillo taught her the basics of how to write in calligraphy. When she saw her student's talent and enjoyment, she encouraged Cathiana to pursue it on her own and even purchased the supplies she needed. Another teacher encouraged her to incorporate her artwork into her history assignments. "Everybody just knew I'm a master with a glue gun," says Cathiana. "I just put a twist on my projects. It makes me happy. Art class grew my passion to be in architecture."

In every way they could, Cathiana's teachers tried to open her eyes to the world outside of East Orange and Newark. When I met Cathiana at the school, we were greeted by Sister Patricia Hogan, who has been the principal at Our Lady for thirty-five years now. A visit from one of her most successful graduates was easily turned into a teachable moment by Sister Pat. She took Cathiana and me to every classroom in the school. Gently pushing us through each door, she explained to class after class of attentive students that Cathiana used to be a student at the school, that she paid attention and did well and went to college. She "made good" and now she was going to be interviewed for a book!

The students looked impressed—a little intimidated even—but Sister Pat wanted to make sure that they had the opportunity to show us what they knew as well. In a kindergarten class, the teacher called students to the blackboard to show us their addition skills. In the upper grades, students told us what they were reading and about some recent writing assignments. As we walked through the halls, Sister Pat didn't hesitate to reprimand students who were not in dress code.

She runs what you might call a tight ship. But she has given her life to the school and Cathiana has a deep appreciation for all of her efforts, marveling at the energy that she could still bring to the job after all these decades. Walking by one of the school's bulletin boards, Cathiana notices an advertisement for a Zumba class to be held there one evening a week. It was Sister Pat's idea. She charges people $10 per class and, after paying the teacher, she manages to keep a few dollars of each fee for the school. Every dollar counts, she tells me, when she can help one of her families pay a little bit less in the way of tuition.

Sister Pat and the other teachers at Our Lady want to make sure that the school is open for students as much as possible. In addition to offering as many activities as they can afford—Girl Scouts, a drum and bugle corps, a variety of sports—the school also opens at 6:45 a.m. each day and provides every student with a full breakfast.

Her teachers tried to give Cathiana and her classmates all the advantages, but they knew there would come a time when she might need a different perspective in order to succeed. They encouraged her to apply for a scholarship to a boarding school when she was going into ninth grade. She got into the program and spent a summer taking courses to better prepare her for it. Ultimately she decided to attend a local Catholic high school instead.

But for college Cathiana was determined to go away. A lot of students—even the best ones—stick close to home after high school. Her older sister stayed home and commuted to Montclair State. Cathiana recalls: "It was like she was suffocating. She couldn't experience the world. The only way you can truly do that is to move onto campus." Cathiana has very clear opinions on this now but she felt this way even in high school. "The only way to really know who you are and become the person that you should be is to cut off ties—not completely—but just move away and see how you're going to deal with it."

Cathiana knows there is often a good reason to stay close by. "If you live in New Jersey and go to a New Jersey school you get a lot of financial aid." And many students need to be concerned about leaving home. She knows of students who have been lured out of state by a lot of financial aid the first year but then the schools scaled back.

As it turned out, Cathiana didn't have to worry. She was the recipient of a Gates Millennial Scholarship. Funded by the Bill and Melinda Gates Foundation, the award covers tuition, room, and board for four years of undergraduate school and a year of graduate school. If you choose to go on for your PhD, that's also covered.

Cathiana's guidance counselor recommended she apply. She completed the application one minute before the midnight deadline, she recalls. A lot of her friends and classmates didn't bother when they saw it was thirty pages long. What kept going through Cathiana's head was something her teachers had always asked her, "What would you do if you couldn't fail?" She thinks: "I could have just been like, there's no way they're going to give me the scholarship. And I wouldn't have done it." But she thought, "What's the worst that could happen if I do it?"

These days, any time she has a doubt, she asks herself those same questions. To be honest, Cathiana says: "I really haven't failed yet. So I'm going to keep going with that same attitude and see what happens."

Cathiana did very well in college, but it wasn't simply because she is smart, though she certainly is. She was well prepared by her Catholic elementary and high schools. "I knew how to write papers. I knew how to deal with my professors," she tells me. What does she mean by that? "You can't shy away from the fact that if you don't understand something you need to talk to the professor." In college, she saw it was something many of her peers were missing. She remembers her seventh grade teacher advising the students not to be embarrassed if they had to ask for help. "You're better off asking for help than struggling by yourself for hours." In college, she said, some of her classmates commented on how she was always meeting with teachers. "If I don't understand something in the one hour of class, I have no problem coming back after school. I just carried that from elementary school to high school to college."

Education Pays

Education really does pay off, and while high school graduates can expect to earn more than high school dropouts, earnings and job prospects for college graduates are significantly better than those with just a high school diploma. Cathiana's master's degree in accounting will likely result in a higher salary and increased lifetime earnings for her. Consider that:

- High school dropouts are three times more likely to be unemployed and more than twice as likely to live in poverty as high school graduates.
- College graduates can expect to earn nearly three times as much as high school dropouts, and twice as much as high school graduates.
- The *Wall Street Journal* recently reported that having a master's degree boosts earnings by as much as 33 percent over employees with a bachelor's degree.

Sources:
http://blogs.wsj.com/economics/2013/04/02/college-grads-earn-nearly-three-times-
    more-than-high-school-dropouts/
http://www.bls.gov/emp/ep_chart_001.htm
http://nces.ed.gov/pubs2012/2012026/tables/table_31a.asp

In high school, Cathiana was deeply immersed in all areas of school life. She played volleyball and softball every year—she would have done basketball too, but her mother thought she should take a break. Instead, she was the manager of the basketball team, helping the other students think about strategy and ways to improve their playing. She was a leader in school competitions. She organized school dances and the prom.

When Cathiana got to college, she quickly realized that it would take some serious discipline and time management in order to get her schoolwork accomplished and take advantage of all the things Syracuse had to offer. If she had a meeting for a club from 7:00 to 9:00 p.m., she would make sure that throughout the day she was doing schoolwork. "Lunch break would be a time not for me to talk to friends. It's for me to go to the library and do my work." After the club's meeting, she recalled, "I would not stay around for too much chit chat."

After her sophomore year in college, Cathiana was offered an internship at PricewaterhouseCoopers and has continued working there each summer until she finished her master's degree. Her mother didn't understand how she could be making so much money when she didn't even have her degree yet.

Cathiana marvels at all of the programs available to help kids who don't know much about college or graduate degrees or professional careers. She got the internship through a program called End Roads that helps match students with different companies. You have to apply for the internship yourself but the program can "vouch for" the students, as Cathiana explains. "It's kind of crazy. I just kept joining programs and these programs kept opening doors for me."

At her Pricewaterhouse internship, Cathiana learned about the different departments at the company, including forensic accounting. "Now that has got to be the coolest accounting in the world," she thought. She laughs. "Typically people don't think accountants are cool. But I had never heard of this." Cathiana sees it as a way to be both "the good guys and the bad guys." On the one hand, they "help companies with profitability by looking through their data and seeing what they're doing wrong or what they're doing right." On the other hand, "we're the people helping the government to find people engaged in fraud and helping them with investigations. The accountant could be called into court to present evidence. I was like, this has just got to be the coolest thing."

Cathiana just started working full time at Pricewaterhouse a couple of months before we meet, but she already has amassed as much time as a second-year associate through her internships. She says her time there "has allowed me to be a leader." She has become the "go-to person for people who just start because it's easier for you to ask someone at your own level for help than to ask someone in a higher level."

One of the most important lessons that Cathiana learned from her teachers at Our Lady Help of Christians is "putting myself in others' shoes." "It's not all about you," she tells me. "That's what they always preached. You should always be willing to help someone because someone was willing to help you." At the end of what are often her very long days on the job, Cathiana always offers to stay later to help. "I know you're going to be working for another five hours. Is there something I can help you with so you can only work three extra hours today?"

A few years ago, Cathiana was asked to be the commencement speaker for eighth-grade graduation at Our Lady Help of Christians. She was thrilled to accept, of course. "I remember sitting in those seats and hearing that person's speech. I asked myself, 'What could I say to those kids that could make a difference?'"

Cathiana is still living at home and she has been offering her younger brother advice about his own career. He's going to school to get a degree in marketing and has been unloading trucks for Macy's over the summer. Cathiana has encouraged him to apply for a job there in marketing when he graduates. "I think he can make that happen," she tells me, with total surety.

Cathiana is a very confident young woman. It's possible to hear the things she says and find her even a little cocky. She has worked hard to get to where she is but she never fails to give credit to her family and all of the teachers and mentors who have helped her get to this point. It is not only the rigorous academic courses she took or even all of the opportunities that her teachers and guidance counselors encouraged her to pursue.

One of Cathiana's favorite memories of school was each day after recess when the whole school would come inside and pray the rosary. She noticed early on that it wasn't Sister Pat who was leading the prayer. There were students elected in the seventh grade to lead it. Being one of those students, Cathiana recalls, "forces you to own it." The daily prayer allowed her to grow in her faith, but it also created a "spiritual bond" with others in her class. Most of all, she recalls the value of prayer in her day. "They turned off the lights so you could really get into it. And then it just calms you down. I don't know. It gives you a whole brand new burst of energy after you do it."

That burst of energy has sustained Cathiana long past recess.

5

A PLACE OF PEACE AMID
A WORLD OF VIOLENCE

Anthony Samuels pictured here with his mother and aunt at a CSF Philadelphia benefit dinner. *Courtesy of CSF Philadelphia.*

Sometimes you just have to take a chance to make things better. That was what Anthony Samuels's mother must have thought when she passed by the Abington Friends School (AFS), a wealthy private institution, on her way from her home in North Philadelphia to her clerical job at Comcast. When Anthony was about to start kindergarten, she pulled onto the lush campus, with its acres of athletic fields and beautifully updated architecture, and walked into the admissions office.

Tuition at Abington Friends, she learned, was about two-thirds of her annual salary. The school admitted Anthony and ended up offering his mother a lot of financial aid—she only paid about half the cost. But after a few years, it was still too much. "My mother loved the school, she loved the atmosphere," Anthony tells me. "She even loved the way I was growing as a person academically. The only thing that could have ended it was the money." Just as she thought she had no choice but to to pull Anthony out of school and send him to a local school in North Philadelphia where they lived, she found out about Children's Scholarship Fund Philadelphia and applied for a scholarship, hoping to keep him at Abington. When his mother found out she was chosen to receive assistance from CSF Philadelphia, Anthony remembers, "it was like a burden was lifted from her shoulders. She literally felt like she hit the lottery."

CSF Philadelphia

Anthony Samuels attended Abington Friends School with a scholarship from CSF Philadelphia (CSFP), a partner program of the national Children's Scholarship Fund. In addition to receiving CSF matching funds, CSFP is also funded by local foundations and individuals, with a significant number of corporate gifts coming through Pennsylvania's Educational Improvement Tax Credit program. CSFP served more than 3,500 Philadelphia children in 2013–2014 and plans to steadily increase the number of new scholarships awarded annually.

Anthony knows what he escaped. A tall young man, with broad shoulders and the slightest remnant of a baby face, Anthony looks relaxed and deeply satisfied coming back to AFS a few years after graduation. But he shakes his head and sighs as he talks about the path he might have gone down.

Many of his peers have been incarcerated and one of his cousins, "who was a great student when he was younger," just returned from serving a ten-year prison sentence. Anthony doesn't want to talk about the details of the crime, but he says, "Even if he didn't have anything to do with it, he just got caught up being around the negativity." Surrounded by violence with no male role models and stuck in schools that are no different from the neighborhoods that surround them, Anthony knows that he could have easily ended up in the same situation as his cousin.

His earliest memories of Abington Friends are that everything "felt bright and brand new." The setting was "warm and friendly and nonviolent." Even at the age of five, Anthony could sense there was something "peaceful" about Abington Friends. Not just because no one was getting into fights with anyone else. There was also a "different level of sophistication" in terms of student interactions with each other.

In his book *The Art of Freedom*, Earl Shorris, who developed a humanities course for underprivileged adults—some of them in prison—describes the effect that a strong liberal arts education can have on individuals. The humanities, he writes, "are a foundation for getting along in the world, for thinking, for learning to reflect on the world instead of just reacting to whatever force is turned against you."

Shorris recounts the story of a young man in his first class—a twenty-four-year-old with a history of violent behavior—who called him describing how a woman at work had provoked him. "She made me so mad, I wanted to smack her up against the wall. I tried to talk to some friends to calm myself down a little, but nobody was around." Shorris asked him what he did, "fearing this was his one telephone call from the city jail." Instead, he told Shorris, "I asked myself, 'What would Socrates do?'"[1]

How do we get kids who are in poor, violent neighborhoods, where every day is just about survival, to think about the long term? How do we get them to consider their own potential? To think about all of the exciting possibilities that the world has to offer them? To act as if the next ten years matter, not just the next ten minutes? The schools that rise to this challenge are the best hope for lifting up underprivileged kids and their families.

Anthony Samuels describes how Abington Friends provided him with an environment in which he could think and talk in peace. "You just don't have dumb conversations here," says Anthony, as he looks around the airy modern library where we're talking. "Any conversation that you have here is going to be useful. Everything that I've learned since first grade is used in college in my everyday life."

Students at the school gather every Wednesday in the Quaker meetinghouse on campus. Sometimes they experience silence together. Other times they discuss a question that affects the community. Even the youngest students participate and discuss issues such as "What makes a good friend?"

Going back and forth between his school and his neighborhood was "like living in two different habitats." Anthony says that it was hard at first, "growing up with a bunch of kids who were out of control and then being here, in a school where everyone was really peaceful and well-spoken and quiet." After being in the school for a few years, he remembers asking his mother why the kids in his neighborhood made fun of the way he spoke.

"That's because you're educated and you'll be the one who is more successful and will be able to go far." Looking back, Anthony says, without not the slightest bit of smugness, "the same ones who were teasing me are the ones who are currently doing prison sentences and whatnot."

Fitting in at Abington was not easy either. There were only a handful of other black students on campus back then. (Today Abington seems quite racially diverse—about a third are students of color—and one of its administrators tells me they have made a significant effort in this regard, recruiting underprivileged and minority students.) But Anthony did have the advantage of starting at AFS early. This meant that unlike some of the other CSF scholarship recipients who may find themselves already academically behind when they start at a private school, Anthony was not trying to make up for any academic deficits.

His fifth-grade teacher, an African American, provided one of the first serious black male role models in his life. "He was an inspiration because I knew he was in my shoes too. He understood my situation."

But he found other teachers at Abington to be deeply nurturing as well. Of one, he says, "she was really peaceful." The word peace comes up again and again during my conversations with Anthony. It's not a coincidence. Abington is a Quaker school and although Anthony does not come from a religious background, he embraced the Quaker values he learned there.

Diversity of Private Schools

Although the phrase "private school" often calls to mind elite schools in bucolic settings (like Anthony Samuels's alma mater, Abington Friends School), more than 5.2 million students (approximately 10 percent of all school-age children in the U.S.) attend a wide variety of private schools, including lower-cost schools in inner-city neighborhoods.

The types of schools private school students attend (2011–2012):

Catholic	42.9%
Nonsectarian	19.8%
Conservative Christian	14.0%
Baptist	4.5%
Lutheran	3.6%
Jewish	5.5%
Episcopal	2.1%
Seventh-day Adventist	1.1%
Calvinist	0.5%
Friends	0.4%

Sources:
http://nces.ed.gov/programs/digest/d11/tables/dt11_003.asp?referrer=report
http://www.capenet.org/facts.html

Peace and friendship were the most important lessons, he says. But students were also taught to have a sense of humility. It is more important "to be part of a community than to just be an individual." Sure, you can pursue your dreams, but if you are focused too much on "standing out in society, the unity is broken."

Anthony Samuels was an enthusiastic student. When we walk into the lobby of AFS, teachers and students converge on him. His classes were small—only about sixteen students each—and even with seven hundred students on campus, it felt like he knew everyone. He recalls teachers whose own kids attended the school and says, "I grew up with them."

It has been awhile since Anthony's come back to visit—the bus ride from North Philadelphia hasn't gotten any shorter—but teachers and even some of the older students remember him fondly and can't wait to catch up on what he's been doing.

After graduating AFS, he went to a small school in Massachusetts called Elms College. He was recruited to play Division III basketball there and received a significant scholarship. He made the Dean's List both semesters of his freshman year. "I was prepared completely," he says with easy confidence. Papers that would have earned Cs from his teachers at AFS were getting him As in college.

He doesn't remember the atmosphere at Abington as particularly harsh when it came to grading. "They just prepare you to meet your best potential. They don't make you feel bad or make you feel dumb, but they let you know that there is still room to improve."

Anthony received only As on his writing assignments freshman year and he had no problem participating in class discussions. Abington's small classes meant that he was "forced to participate and be involved and really lock on to what's going on academically."

Some of his college teammates were not as lucky. In addition to everything else that AFS provided, Anthony said he learned how to stay organized in school—to be able to participate in sports and multiple extracurricular activities, while at the same time ensuring that his academic pursuits didn't falter.

When he got to college, he says, "it wasn't that I was smarter than everyone else. I was just more well organized than my peers, and certainly more well organized than anyone on the basketball team." He knew how to take notes in class in a way that reminded him what was important later on when he was studying for an exam or completing a writing assignment. This is a skill that many college professors will readily tell you many students are lacking.

But after a year, Anthony was homesick and he didn't think much of the academic environment at Elms. He figured the time was right to transfer to a more prestigious school and "take my academics more seriously." So he stopped playing basketball and transferred to Temple University, where his mother had recently taken a job. He has a 3.0 average now but he is working his way back up and feels that he is learning much more than he was last year. Anthony is scheduled to graduate from Temple in the spring of 2014 with a degree in account-ing.

Finances, though, are still a struggle for Anthony and his mother. It is easy to see how being surrounded by the kind of money at Abington Friends or any of the other more wealthy schools profiled in this book could breed a kind of resentment in kids from more modest backgrounds, but this generally doesn't seem to happen.

When Anthony would visit his friends' homes, he would often ask the kids what their parents did for a living. "I was inspired by them. It was where I wanted to be someday." Both financially and otherwise, Anthony says that being at Abington Friends "molds you and builds you up to want to be better. There is just a different level of ambition that I have."

After his senior year of high school, Anthony gave a speech at a Children's Scholarship Fund Philadelphia event and he was offered two summers of internships at Coca-Cola. He went on to get another internship at a different Fortune 500 company, this time in accounts payable. He is hoping that these kinds of résumé-building positions will help him to get a good job when he graduates.

Ultimately, he decided to study accounting because he wanted to understand "everything that goes on in business, how it operates." He tells me that he wants to "put myself in a situation where I could send my kids here and have a big crib and drive a nice car."

"That's my goal, to be extremely successful and just help people who came from the same situation as me. I would get a kid from public school and invest in his education. . . . If more people would get the opportunity I was given, the world would be a better place."

When Anthony gets a job, though, he plans to donate money for scholarships so that others who are in his position can attend schools like Abington Friends. "That's my goal," he says, "to be extremely successful and just help people who came from the same situation as me. I would get a kid from public school and invest in his education. A lot of people would love the opportunity. If I could change ten people's lives, I would be content with myself," says Anthony. "If more people would get the opportunity I was given, the world would be a better place."

While a student at AFS, Anthony was involved in a variety of public service projects from Habitat for Humanity to the Special Olympics. But unlike many students who leave such activities behind once they are otherwise occupied with college, Anthony has continued to volunteer in his old neighborhood. He helps out at the Hank Gathers Recreation Center in Philadelphia. Though he'll sometimes play basketball with the kids, he wants them to know that sports are not the key to their success.

"I told them that academics is everything." These kids are under the impression that professional sports are a viable route out of the ghetto. Anthony tells them that their schoolwork is what they should be focused on. Basketball is a nice way to keep kids off the street, but it's not going to solve the deeper problems that face them—the poor schools in their neighborhood and the lack of opportunity to advance.

Anthony is deeply grateful to AFS and CSF Philadelphia for solving these problems in his life. But he is always quick to give credit where it is due. "I was very fortunate to have a mother who put my education first." It was Anthony's mother who took the initiative when he was young, knocking on the door at AFS. Children's Scholarship Fund was ultimately a vehicle, a way that Anthony's mother could be empowered to make the right decisions for her son's education.

6

"LITTLE HOUSE ON THE PRAIRIE"

Aleysha Taveras with her brother, Gabriel, and mother, Gloria Vargas, at her high school graduation from Academy of Mount St. Ursula in the Bronx in 2012. *Courtesy of Children's Scholarship Fund.*

Gloria Vargas worked as a teacher's aide and a parent coordinator at her neighborhood public school in the South Bronx. She quickly learned from that school exactly what she didn't want in a school for her daughter, Aleysha. Everyone in her neighborhood, Aleysha says, "knew that the public school wasn't a place you could thrive." But Gloria had first-hand experience. She knew the things that other parents didn't know, the things kids tried to hide from their families about gangs and violence. She knew about classes where nothing was being learned and students who didn't bother to tell anyone. She saw kids struggling in large unruly classes, and parents who were helpless to change things.

Aleysha's mother decided to send her to St. John Chrysostom School and paid the tuition on her own until Aleysha was in fourth grade and her brother was in second. Then she couldn't afford it anymore and found out about Children's Scholarship Fund and applied for a scholarship. Before that it was always a "struggle." Between Aleysha's tuition and her brother's "it was most of her paycheck."

Like Gloria, many mothers and fathers are referred to CSF by family, friends, or neighbors. Others find out about it when they go to the school they are interested in. Some hear about CSF in church. The application process is relatively simple. Parents either send in their tax return, or, if they don't file taxes, a variety of income-related documents. CSF's guidelines for determining whether a family is eligible are based on the federal government's free- and reduced-lunch program rules. Parents simultaneously apply to the school they want their children to attend and to the scholarship program. They are told they will have to pay the balance between the tuition and the scholarship, with a minimum family contribution of $500.

Gloria Vargas would have happily jumped through many more hoops than that to make sure her daughter was able to attend St. John. Aleysha arrived at the school some mornings before 7:00 a.m. since her mother had to be at work early.

Gloria wanted many things from a school, but mostly, says her daughter, "She wanted teachers who would always be on top of me." Aleysha's mother was born in Puerto Rico to a very faithful Catholic family and so the religious environment of the school was important to her as well. In both the religious and academic mission of the school, Gloria wanted teachers who would be working with her to fulfill her dreams for her daughter. "I didn't want her to be like me," says Gloria. "To struggle as a single parent to pay the bills."

To meet Aleysha today, it is hard to imagine that any parent would ever worry about her or think that teachers needed to ask her twice to do anything. She is a paragon of self-discipline. At the age of nineteen, she carries herself like someone much older. She is well spoken and confident.

Children are not born like this, of course. Many stray, and many more simply don't reach their full potential. But Aleysha, one feels confident, will accomplish a lot, and that is at least in part thanks to the support she received from Children's Scholarship Fund.

Aleysha and I meet on a mild fall afternoon in the main office of St. John Chrysostom School. School is off for teacher meetings. A janitor is doing some painting downstairs to keep the old building looking neat and clean. Hard to believe now, but the church, which was founded in 1896, was originally in a grassy pasture. As waves of immigrants moved in, the neighborhood was built up, first by Jews, then by the Irish. The school was constructed in 1914 and by the 1940s had an enrollment that topped one thousand students. In the 1950s and 1960s, Hispanics from Puerto Rico and the Dominican Republic began to arrive.

In the late 1960s and 1970s, the neighborhood experienced a precipitous fall. Many of the buildings surrounding St. John Chrysostom went up in flames. During the 1970s and 1980s, Hoe Avenue & 167th Street was considered part of the "Fort Apache" section of the South Bronx. St. John became a safe haven for neighborhood children, even referred to as "Little House on the Prairie." As a result of its history, the school has maintained its mission of "excellence in a nonviolent atmosphere."

Today, the neighborhood doesn't pose the same physical dangers it once did. Police cars and foot patrols regularly go by the school's parking lot. An ice cream truck is parked around the corner with a few people lined up quietly waiting for milk shakes. As in much of New York, the quality of life in the South Bronx has improved but the schools have remained a problem.

The receptionists in the office at St. John are thrilled to see Aleysha and rush to embrace her when she walks in. She is a freshman now at Seton Hall University just across the river in New Jersey. She comes home on most weekends but her mother doesn't live close to the school now and Aleysha doesn't get back to see her alma mater as much as she used to.

But anyone who has known Aleysha would be hard pressed to forget her. She is sweet and bubbly. Her long strands of curly hair bounce around her face. Her smile is inviting.

What she remembers most about St. John is its warmth and its structure. "The teachers were always kind," she tells me, looking around the small gymnasium she used to play in with her friends. With sixty kids in a grade, everyone knew everyone else. At St. John, Aleysha's teachers nurtured her. Her best friend from kindergarten to this day was the daughter of two of the school's teachers. They became "like a second family" to her.

The atmosphere was not particularly strict, but "with every teacher we had, we knew what they expected of us. This is what we did every day. We had order. We had a schedule." Aleysha had a difficult time when her parents were going through a divorce. Gloria Vargas remembers that her daughter "was always nervous, biting her nails and pulling her hair." The teachers at St. John "helped her focus and concentrate. They were able to channel those nerves into reading and other things." They also helped her "discover she was a great writer. They really pushed my daughter."

Gloria emphasizes how "lucky" her family has been and how "grateful" she is "for the good people who helped me mold Aleysha into what she is now." She says, "I see first-hand how kids in the school system don't make it. I don't have that worry."

Some people assume that going to Catholic school means "you can't step out of line," says Aleysha, but she thinks "the teachers understood that we would make mistakes and we would need to learn from them. They were there to teach us what we should have done."

Though Aleysha came from a fairly stable home, some of her friends did not. One, she recalls, was always going back and forth between living with her mother and her father. "I feel like school gave her at least something stable. She always came here. No matter what, her parents kept her here, even when there was a lot of stuff going on in her life."

Since she graduated, Aleysha says she has met people her age who did not have that kind of structure when they were young and it presented problems for them in college. They were not able to create the kind of order they needed on their own. College, as most educators would agree, demands time-management skills. Students who have not been inculcated with these habits early are more likely to fall behind in their studies. Even if they have the other intellectual tools to get on well, college offers the kind of freedom (freedom to attend classes or not, freedom to study for exams, freedom to take on extracurricular activities, etc.) that requires maturity to handle.

College and Career Readiness

Aleysha's academic background gave her a strong foundation for college, and her work experience with the National Park Service has prepared her for a post-college career. However, many American teens are leaving high school without the basic skills necessary to succeed in college or in the workforce. In Aleysha's hometown of New York City, on-time high school graduation rates for African American and Hispanic students are 55 percent and 52.7 percent, respectively. Yet, among the students who do graduate, only 22.2 percent meet the state's definition for being college-ready. Only 25 percent of American teens taking the ACT test in 2012 scored well enough to be considered college ready in English, reading, mathematics, and science. For African American and Hispanic teens, the numbers were even lower (5 percent and 11 percent respectively).

Sources:
http://schools.nyc.gov/Accountability/data/GraduationDropoutReports/default.htm
http://media.act.org/documents/CCCR12-NationalReadinessRpt.pdf

"Life on campus is definitely different from living at home. You have so much freedom," Aleysha tells me excitedly. But then she stops herself. "I don't want to say that. I can't just call it freedom because you have to set your time when you wake up every morning. You have to budget your time, make lists." She says her college professors "are very nice. They're understanding." On the other hand, she says, "it's up to you. You don't have to come to class. That's on you, you know."

Her teachers in elementary school and high school, she says, "taught me how to be organized. This is where I'm owning my skills."

A few years ago, David Brooks wrote a piece for the *Atlantic* called "The Organization Kid," in which he described the overscheduled lives of college students today. At Princeton, he says,

> I asked several students to describe their daily schedules, and their replies sounded like a session of Future Workaholics of America: crew practice at dawn, classes in the morning, resident advisor duty, lunch, study groups, classes in the afternoon, tutoring disadvantaged kids in Trenton, a cappella practice, dinner, study, science lab, prayer session, hit the StairMaster, study a few hours more.

But even at schools that are not in the Ivy League, the most successful students are the ones who work hard and know how to squeeze everything in. Time and again, CSF scholarship recipients say that they appreciate the sense of order and structure they have learned and talk about how it has served them well in college and in their careers afterwards.

In school, Aleysha's two favorite subjects were religion and history. Her seventh- and eighth-grade teachers at St. John made these subjects "so interesting for me." They formed the basis for her current interest in diplomacy and international relations. Much of what you need to know about understanding the relationships between countries comes from history. "But it's also culture and religion and government."

Every subject that Aleysha studied at St. John seemed to expand her horizons. She recalls a math class in which her teachers asked them to pick a place in the United States they would like to travel to, somewhere far away. They were asked to "plan a journey, calculate how much money we would need, how much we would pay for gas, for the hotel and all that stuff." Aleysha still remembers that because "it made me think it would be kind of cool to travel. It would be expensive but it would be a really great adventure." For students like Aleysha, who rarely left their neighborhoods growing up, having teachers who encouraged them to think about the world outside proved extremely important.

In seventh grade, Aleysha was faced with the question of where to attend high school. Most of her classmates were going to one Catholic high school but her mother encouraged her to explore all her options. She did well on a science exam and was accepted into an intensive science program for high school. But she didn't like the atmosphere of the school—she found it a little "dark and dingy." So she visited the Academy of Mount St. Ursula, near Fordham University. In addition to a strong academic reputation, Aleysha was attracted by all of the sports and extracurricular activities the school offered.

Even when she was younger Aleysha's mother tried to keep her and her younger brother very busy. She was in swimming, Tae Kwon Do, guitar classes, and on Friday nights she practiced with the church choir.

The combination of all of these activities and the hard work she had to do at St. John, Aleysha says, were a good preparation for high school. She already knew how to write an essay, which, she says, a lot of her classmates did not. Her teachers made her write a lot. When she started high school, she remembers thinking, "I had a one-up on everyone."

Aleysha said she worked hard and was always a straight-A student. Her teachers probably could have just let her be and she would have turned out fine but they always wanted to find new ways to challenge her.

In eighth grade, Aleysha told one of her teachers at St. John that she wanted to be an early childhood teacher. "I don't think you want to do that," the teacher replied. She meant no disrespect to preschool teachers, of course. But she wanted Aleysha to consider other possibilities. She offered Aleysha a job at one of the school's summer programs for small children. "If you like it afterward," she said, "then you do it." Aleysha's teacher was right. Working with small children is one of those things you have to be called to do. It shouldn't just be a default job for working-class young women who get good grades. And Aleysha realized after that summer that it was not what she wanted to do.

Both at St. John and Mount St. Ursula, teachers were always encouraging her to apply for other programs and internships. "If you want to do it, if you like it," they would tell Aleysha, "then do it." She tells me, "They pushed us into these kinds of programs and they love to hear about these things."

The summer between her sophomore and junior years of high school, she applied to be an intern for the National Park Service (NPS). Two of her friends were going to apply as well and she thought, "It sounded kind of interesting." After a week-long environmental education program, the NPS would consider whether to offer you a job for the remainder of the summer. Aleysha shadowed a national park ranger and got to visit all of the different venues in the area to learn about them.

But what does a national park ranger do in New York? Ellis Island, the Statue of Liberty, and Governor's Island are all federal parklands, Aleysha explains. Guides spend most of their time explaining the history of these sites. The following year, Aleysha returned to the NPS, this time as an assistant to the business manager of the local sites. She went to work every day at Federal Hall on Wall Street, the building in which George Washington took his oath of office and where the first government of the United States was housed. Aleysha says it was "awesome to be in that building, but also to develop those kinds of connections" with the people she worked for. Her boss even offered her a college recommendation.

The following summer she was based at Governor's Island working on an education project for a new exhibit there. She was able to order things for the exhibit herself. "They trusted me even though I was an intern. I got to wear a uniform." The program led her to parts of the city she would have never thought to visit at all, let alone regularly. She learned about the history of the city she loved and the people who lived here before her.

This program she applied for on a whim now "just falls into my whole history," Aleysha tells me. Her teachers were very supportive of all her endeavors. "They think it's really cool that I'm a park ranger. They love seeing us do these kinds of things."

During her junior year of high school, she attended the National Youth Leadership Forum in Washington, DC, a program for which her teachers had to write recommendations. She stayed there by herself for a week to learn about careers in the FBI, the CIA, and the National Guard, among other things. "It was a really good experience to find out what you wanted to do."

In high school, Aleysha began to envision herself becoming an ambassador, negotiating peace treaties between different countries. "That was the ideal." Now that she is in college and thinking about these things more seriously, she says she plans to start by becoming a foreign service officer. She is talking about the classes she needs to take in order to prepare for the foreign service exam. And while it might seem overwhelming to some, Aleysha can barely contain her enthusiasm. "So I'm going to have to become really fantastic," she jokes with me.

For a high school student in the South Bronx, even an honors student, these are not the kinds of career possibilities that readily present themselves. For Aleysha, attending this conference helped her see her path to college more clearly. "My mom and I realized that we should look for schools that have a government or diplomacy program." She started applying to colleges that had good reputations in international relations

Aleysha applied early decision to Georgetown but her application was deferred. Then she got into her second choice, Seton Hall, which is also a Catholic university. The academic program appealed to her and so did the atmosphere. "It had this little campus feel, but it wasn't too far from the city." She loved the town too, with its cobblestone streets. "It's the stuff you don't see everywhere."

The honors program at Seton Hall has brought Aleysha into some interesting academic settings. A course she is taking now on English and religion has her studying texts from Hinduism, Buddhism, and Christianity. The study of these other faiths is interesting to her but she has also found it remarkable that the other students in her class seem totally unfamiliar with various passages in the Bible, let alone basic doctrines of Catholicism. "I thought it was common knowledge," says Aleysha. College has been a "reality check" on this front and has made her a little "uncomfortable" to find herself in such a "non-Catholic" environment. But it has also made her appreciate the strength of the foundation she was given when she was young.

Despite the fact that most of the students at Seton Hall come from a different background, Aleysha has never felt out of place academically or even socially. She took Advanced Placement English and Composition when she was a senior in high school. When her college professors assigned papers, she said, "A lot of people were kind of like, 'We don't know how to do that. It will take us days.'" But Aleysha hasn't had any problems.

It is not uncommon these days for good colleges to try to recruit talented children from poorer neighborhoods. Unfortunately, it also is not uncommon to find that the students who are the recipients of these outreach efforts do not stay in school. They are often underprepared academically and socially, and even if they stay in school, they may scale back their academic expectations, choosing easier majors or dropping out of honors classes.

For those who are concerned about students such as Aleysha reaching their full potential, it is important not only that they be admitted to college but that they complete it and do well there. That means preparing them early for academic success. Data from the National Center for Education Statistics shows that students who had attended private school in eighth grade were twice as likely as those who attended public school to have completed a bachelor's or higher degree by their mid-twenties.

Aleysha not only did well in elementary and secondary school relative to her peers, she also was challenged. She was required to do the kind of writing and math and science that her counterparts at quality suburban public schools do.

Aleysha's grades remain high at Seton Hall. Like many of her peers in CSF programs, Aleysha has been well prepared to enter a college environment. Even socially, she seems to have been imbued with the confidence necessary to compete at an elite school and go into a rigorous profession.

When I ask Aleysha whether she is ever bothered by the fact that most of her classmates come from upper-middle-class backgrounds, she answers by telling me about the things they have in common. "I don't know how they put us together," she says of her roommates, but one of their fathers and one of their mothers have passed away. So growing up with a single parent is something that they share. But with her other roommates, she says, "I do fine with them too. It's not so different. It's not like I see anyone as arrogant. I don't think anyone is so different from me or that they look at me differently."

And why should they? Aleysha has clearly overcome any obstacles she faced as a child and, with a little help toward paying her tuition, she is prepared for college and whatever comes afterward.

POSTSCRIPT

A year after our first meeting, Aleysha had left Seton Hall. Living on campus was simply too expensive for her family. So she transferred to Manhattan College, a private Catholic school in the city, and moved back home. At the same time, she began to rethink her plans to go into diplomacy. Instead, she is majoring in secondary education and social studies. She would probably have a harder time getting into foreign service from a less prestigious school and it may be that education is her vocation after all. She says that her jobs with the National Park Service allowed her to plan exhibits and lessons for students, something she has very much enjoyed. "In my education classes," Aleysha tells me, "we are trying to figure out why our subject matters." But that is something she has already learned. All of those classes she took in international relations, she says, will "help me connect with the students."

Scholarship recipients, like any kids, do not always walk a straight path in life. They can escape their circumstances to a large extent, but the fact that their families don't have money will probably continue to affect them even once they make it to college. That being said, Aleysha is obviously in a much better position than she would have been without the educational opportunities she has had through her CSF scholarship. And if she is able to carry her passion for politics and international relations into a high school classroom, so much the better for the next generation.

7

SIZING UP THE COMPETITION—AND THEN WINNING IT

Julio Barrientos in downtown San Francisco during a break from his job at Citi-bank. *Courtesy of Epoch Times.*

Talking to low-income parents who scraped enough money together to send their kids to private schools, it is easy to forget exactly what was sacrificed in the process. Julio Barrientos, the child of a Peruvian mother and a Guatemalan father, says his immigrant parents disagreed about the importance of private schools for Julio and his younger brother. His mother was all for it. She worried about the public school environment, both in terms of academics and of the "values" that might be imparted there. His father, though, was worried about saving money.

And why shouldn't he be? He was a construction worker, always doing side jobs to make ends meet, and Julio's mother was a babysitter. Neither spoke English. They both came to this country at the age of twenty. Their economic situation was (and still is) precarious. It would be hard to criticize the Barrientos family had they decided to skip private education for their children and instead squirrel away some money in case one of them lost a job or some other unforeseen circumstance occurred.

But Julio's mother was determined. "She really pushed for me. No matter how they did it," Julio tells me, "she wanted me to get into a private school because she really valued education." After thirteen years of Catholic school and a degree from the University of Southern California in business administration, Julio is taking a short break from his first full-time job at Citibank in the heart of San Francisco to talk to me about his childhood and his education.

The BASIC Fund

The BASIC Fund was founded in 1998 by Jim McCarthy, Arthur Rock, and Children's Scholarship Fund (CSF) cofounder John Walton to help low-income families afford the cost of tuition at private schools in the Bay Area. The BASIC Fund has partnered with CSF since 1999, receiving matching funds from CSF for Bay Area scholarships. Since 1998, more than seventeen thousand local children, including Julio Barrientos and his brother, have used BASIC Fund scholarships. The fund boasts a 95 percent high school graduation rate.

Julio is a bear of a guy with an easy laugh. He is wearing a dark suit but seems relaxed as we chat in the lobby of his building. Thanks to the BASIC Fund, a private scholarship program for low-income kids in the city and partner program of the national Children's Scholarship Fund, and the contributions from his parents that were not easy to make, Julio was able to receive the kind of education that is typically reserved for the children of wealthy professionals, not struggling immigrants. He practically gushes as he describes all of the teachers, administrators, and family who helped him get this far.

The Catholic school he attended from kindergarten through eighth grade, Mission Dolores, was not very close to the neighborhood where he grew up. It was about a half an hour in the car each morning. But he had a cousin there, and his grandmother belonged to the parish, so his parents decided that was where he'd go. Julio didn't know a lot of kids who went to the public school that was across the street from his house. But his mother, he said, was aware of the "distractions and the risks" of that school. And Julio knew it could be "dangerous."

Julio's memories of Mission Dolores are enormously happy. He remembers small classes with caring teachers. In second grade, Julio recalls he drew a picture of his house. His teacher, who knew that his mother had just had a baby, offered to drive him home that afternoon. She wanted to meet Julio's new brother but she also wanted to help out the family in any way she could. "The bonds with the teachers were really close."

He remembers a music teacher too—"She could be strict, but there was a joy in her"—and a history teacher who showed him why he should care about her subject. Julio acknowledges that regardless of the grade, he was "always the teacher's pet."

The school felt like a second family to him and to this day, he says, he thinks of his classmates "like brothers and sisters." The classes were small and, he says, "we got to know each other so well for so long." He recently attended a reunion and he says the friendships he made at Mission Dolores "were one of the greatest things about the school." The school enrolled students from a variety of backgrounds. Julio estimates it was about half Hispanic, another 20 percent white, and the rest "a mix of African American, Asian, and everything else." He tells me, "we got along great." With the guys, he doesn't remember there being different "cliques."

"We just had a good time together." Julio remembers how much "fun" Mission Dolores was. The teachers threw the kids parties for reading a certain number of books. The seventh graders regularly read to the first graders. There was a sense of the older kids taking care of the younger ones.

Like many young boys, Julio had a competitive streak. Thankfully this was nurtured in the right ways at school. He remembers playing "Around the World" with math equations. "It was a race to solve them," he recalls. "If the person who is standing up wins, they go on to the next stage; they go 'around the world' and get a stamp on their index card." Julio smiles as he tells me with lingering satisfaction, "I remember having this whole card full of stamps."

Despite the fact that he worked so hard in school, he assures me that he was "never picked on or teased for being smart." He thinks there may have been some jealousy over the attention he sometimes received, but his classmates were "really supportive."

Activities like "Around the World," along with the kindness of his classmates, gave Julio the confidence he needed to succeed in later grades. Julio continued to excel at math throughout his elementary and high school years and he also continued to compete with his classmates and others through the academic decathlons he entered. Mission Dolores went head-to-head against other schools in the area. Julio also ran for a variety of student government offices, and he was elected treasurer and vice president. The competition was hardly cutthroat, but Julio clearly enjoys winning.

Reading and writing were not his favorite subjects. Which is to say, when he got a grade lower than an A, a rare occurrence, it would have been in English. Julio learned to read at the same time as his classmates but, he says, when he got into the later grades, he just seemed to have a smaller vocabulary than some of them so he had to work harder.

Julio says his teachers not only expected him to work hard, they also taught him *how* to work hard. He emphasized the "study skills" he gained at Mission Dolores. "When you got home, you did your homework first. You had to really organize yourself" in order to accomplish all the reading that would be assigned. Maybe it sounds obvious, but Julio says, "To me, someone's future starts as a kid. I know there are a lot of people who can turn themselves around, but for me it really helped that I established a solid start from the beginning."

Julio says he had "no idea what college was" when he was at Mission Dolores but his teachers did, and they "forced him to do well in school to get into a great high school," which eventually put him on the right path to college. In fact, Mission Dolores helped him significantly with that process. Julio received a full scholarship to one of the best and most expensive high schools in the city. (Tuition is now a little less than $40,000 a year.)

Stuart Hall High School is a Catholic school located in San Francisco's Pacific Heights District, and every year they offer a full scholarship to a worthy student. The scholarship is funded by the school's alumni. Julio recalls that he had to write an essay about "religious values" for the competition. His teachers and his principal also wrote recommendations for him. It helped, he says, that they knew him so well.

Because of his education at Mission Dolores, Julio was able to compete with the kids at Stuart Hall, most of who had been educated at highly competitive public and private elementary schools in the city and were headed to some of the best colleges in the country. At first, he was surprised by the money at Stuart Hall. "It was a struggle coming from a poor background." The parents drove Mercedes. Julio remembers a couple of Lamborghinis as well. He wondered what the parents did. "Being exposed to that pushed me—not in an evil greedy way," Julio assures me. "I just wanted to prove that someone can make themselves into a successful person."

In high school, Julio earned a 3.8 GPA. He also threw himself into extracurricular activities. Though many young people will happily recite their high school résumé to anyone who asks, Julio talks mostly about how much the teachers there gave to him and how much he loved the experience of being at Stuart Hall. When you ask about what he did in high school, he strays off the topic easily. But when you add it all up, it's hard to imagine how Julio managed it.

He ran cross country and played lacrosse. (Julio jokes that he weighed a little less back then. Banking is not quite as much exercise.) He was the vice president of his senior class and the class representative for the years prior to that. He was in the school musical and even choreographed some of the dancing.

He also participated in the school's extensive community service program. He served at a soup kitchen that was located across the street from his home. And he volunteered as an assistant at Rosa Parks Elementary School in a second-grade classroom. "That was to help low-income families and kids," Julio says. "It was a really good experience."

He would go back to Mission Dolores to help out there too. He taught the eighth graders a salsa dance one year for the school's international dinner. And he even coached his younger brother's basketball team. Like many of the other kids who attend private schools on scholarship, Julio started "giving back" even before he had received all of the benefits of the gifts that had been bestowed on him. The importance of service to community had been impressed upon him from a very young age. He knew what he was supposed to do and why.

Paying It Forward

Julio Barrientos, himself only a recent college graduate, is already helping his parents out with his younger brother's high school tuition. Like many of the scholarship alumni interviewed in this book, Julio appreciates that others have helped him, and he plans to donate to the scholarship fund that assisted him so other young people get the same start he did. Julio's altruism is backed up by research from a team from Case Western Reserve University, which found that children who received a scholarship were significantly more likely to be altruistic towards charitable organizations than children who had not been awarded a scholarship.

Source:
http://www.nber.org/papers/w11725.pdf

With academics, though, it was different. He wanted to please his teachers and his parents, but he didn't really have any long-term understanding of his education. When he was a junior in high school and met for the first time with a college counselor, things started to get a little clearer. But he had never set foot on a college campus. He didn't know which schools were the good ones. He'd heard of Harvard and Stanford, but that was about it. "I saw what my friends were doing. They already knew about it because their parents went to college." (He tells me that Stuart Hall now starts the college process much earlier in high school.)

A friend of his from China told him that he was applying to the University of Southern California to study business. So Julio applied there too. In all, he sent applications to fifteen schools and was accepted at thirteen of them. "It was really fun, an exciting time. The best feeling is the acceptance letters would come and my mom . . . we were going crazy every time the letters would come in." His letter from USC is framed in the kitchen.

Still, the first time Julio went to a college was when he went to college. He can still recall the first time he "saw the big statues and the entranceway." He recalls, "I was just so amazed." His father helped him move all of his stuff into his dorm with his construction truck. Both of his parents were "very proud," says Julio.

Julio studied hard in college, but he acknowledges there were a lot of distractions when he was a freshman. He did join a fraternity early on but quickly decided that it was not a priority. He wanted to have some fun in college, but mostly, Julio knew, it was about preparing for a career. He had always worked while he went to school. "If I wanted something, I had to work for it," he recalls. In high school he was a receptionist for the church at Mission Dolores on the weekends. In college he had a work-study job on campus and during the summers he held internships. One summer, he worked at MetLife and the summer before he graduated he got a job at Citibank.

He's in an entry-level position there now, working as the executive assistant to the regional manager and director. He doesn't have a designated field yet but he is being exposed to a variety of different options in his current position.

Even though he has a girlfriend back in Los Angeles, Julio decided it was important to move back home to help out his family. His parents divorced when he was a senior in high school so he has always tried to be a big presence in his younger brother's life.

His brother has followed in his footsteps, attending Mission Dolores (which has since merged with another Catholic elementary school) and then Stuart Hall. His brother received a BASIC Fund scholarship as well, for kindergarten through eighth grade. Julio says his parents never would have been able to send two kids to private school without it. And his brother now gets a lot of financial aid at Stuart Hall, but because he did not win the same scholarship as Julio, his parents must pay significantly more themselves.

Julio is helping out with the tuition bills. "I want to help him get a better education." Julio recalls that when he was growing up (and his parents were still together) he had their full support. His mother helped him with homework when he was young, but things have been different for his brother. Their father has been out of work and his mother can't help as much. Julio says that his brother "never had so much attention. I'm kind of worried he doesn't stick to it. That's why I stayed here."

Some of Julio's friends from childhood have had trouble sticking to it. Some finished Mission Dolores but then went on to high school and got off track. Some dropped out of high school. Others finished but didn't have the skills to do well in college. Some are in community college now part time. "I always think that the key to success is you've got to do well in the beginning so you can do better in the next stage and the next stage. Or else you'll fall behind." Now that his friends are adults, they have to balance their desire to finish their education with their need to make money. "They don't have the resources now."

Julio hopes that his brother can benefit from some of the things Julio has learned. The high schooler has already visited USC a few times. "He has a greater advantage," says Julio, because he has been planning to go to college all along.

Julio says that he hopes he can help other kids in addition to his brother benefit from his experience. For one thing, he plans to donate to the BASIC Fund once he is done helping with his brother's tuition bills. "I want to help other people who are in a similar situation to what I was, who can make it in life but they don't have all the resources." Julio plans to give to his schools as well and to a program called A Better Chance (ABC) that helped him with his college application essays.

He knows that he owes his success to the many adults who watched over him all those years. From the teachers at Mission Dolores who instilled in him a love of learning to the teachers at Stuart Hall who constantly asked if he needed help with his work, Julio thinks about them all. But it was his mother's realization that he could get the "ethical and the educational values" in Catholic schools that really put Julio on his current path. And soon he hopes his brother will join him.

8

THE BURDENS OF ADULTHOOD, PLACED ON A CHILD

College student and former scholarship recipient Mira Martinez. *Courtesy of the Martinez family.*

Edelmira Blanca Martinez dreams of becoming a pediatric nurse some day. "I want to work with babies and make them feel better. I want to feed them when they need to be fed and give them medicine when they're in pain." Though Mira, as she likes to be called, clearly loves working with children, she does not want any of her own. "I already have my own babies—my siblings." Now a freshman at the Community College of Denver, Mira has four younger brothers and sisters—ages ten, eight, six, and one. Since she was in middle school, she has helped to care for them, acting as a "second mom" to them while her own mother worked long hours to support all of them. Neither her father nor her siblings' father was in the picture.

Mira meets me in the offices of ACE Scholarships, a partner of Children's Scholarship Fund in Denver that offers scholarships to disadvantaged kids between kindergarten and twelfth grade to attend private schools, which has allowed her to overcome these circumstances and put her on the path to a promising career and a stable income. Mira has long, dark, straight hair. She is wearing a white blouse with a belt wrapped around it and a pair of ballet flats. She is quiet but articulate. Her even tone is broken only once toward the end of our conversation when she begins to cry.

ACE Scholarships

Edelmira Martinez is one of more than ten thousand children who have attended private school in Denver with assistance from ACE Scholarships since it was established in 2000. In 2002, ACE became a Children's Scholarship Fund partner program and receives matching funds from the national organization, leveraging its strong base of local support. ACE's annual spring luncheons, which have attracted thousand-plus crowds, have brought national education figures including Geoffrey Canada, Michelle Rhee, and former Florida governor Jeb Bush to Denver. In addition to its Denver scholarships, ACE also runs a statewide scholarship program in Montana.

Mira grew up in the Globeville section of Denver, a formerly industrial neighborhood that has been cut off from the rest of the city by two interstate highways. The smelting companies that used to operate there left behind a mess of contaminated soil and groundwater. The crime rates are significantly higher than the city's averages. Globeville has historically been a neighborhood that attracted immigrant groups and today it has a largely Hispanic population. As the education system has deteriorated, it has become increasingly hard for kids like Mira to learn what they need to and end the cycle of poverty into which they have been born.

Mira describes chaos at Garden Place Academy, the neighborhood elementary school she attended for several years. Even if just a couple of the kids weren't paying attention, the teacher was unable to control the class. "The whole class would get distracted and we'd have to start over. There were times we couldn't even read because there was a student who didn't want to settle down. It was just horrible."

Denver is not the first place that comes to mind when people think of poverty and disadvantage in America. James Coleman, who was also an ACE recipient as well as the alumni coordinator at ACE, grew up in a historically black section of Denver. His grandfather was a preacher there. Some of his friends went on to find success in life, but he says, "I could tell you the names of guys who are dead." He says, "I don't live in the Bronx, I don't live in Compton. I don't live in New Orleans. But there are some real ghettoes here. There are some communities that are truly underserved here."

When Mira was about to enter seventh grade, her mother applied for her to go to Annunciation Catholic School. Her family is Catholic and her mother thought that a religious environment would be preferable. She and her mother were attracted to the smaller classes and the "individualized attention from teachers who actually know your name and your background."

Carlos Hernandez, who does Hispanic outreach for ACE, says that many of the parents who come here "learn about private schools, but conclude they must be extremely expensive." Or they just don't want to ask questions because of the language barrier. "They worry they are going to be put on the spot and they don't want to be ridiculed."

There was no way Mira's family could afford to send her to Catholic school and so the principal of Annunciation recommended they apply for an ACE scholarship. Despite its generosity in giving away more than $20 million in scholarships since its inception, ACE Scholarships has had to turn away many deserving children, as many as six thousand, due to lack of funds. "Thankfully," says Mira, "I got accepted."

Mira liked everything about Annunciation. Even the uniforms. "Going to a public school, it was all about the latest things, who has this and that." Mira's family could hardly afford to keep up with the trends so she was happy to be relieved of that pressure. She liked other aspects of the structure as well. Her friends in public school had been allowed to pick some of their classes. But Mira said, "at Annunciation, they gave us specific classes. We didn't have a choice. I liked that because they're making sure we are taking the classes we need and not wasting time."

She could not afford to waste time. When Mira arrived at Annunciation, she was already two grade levels behind in mathematics. The school agreed to let her into the seventh grade but only if she stayed after school regularly for tutoring. Her teachers devoted long hours to making sure Mira caught up. In reading, meanwhile, she was getting by, but Annunciation really lit a fire under her. Students were encouraged to read books on their own, and after the class completed a certain number, they got a pizza party.

When Mira was in third grade, her mother started talking to her about the importance of going to college. Her mother, who grew up in the same neighborhood, barely finished high school. Mira was born when her mother was twenty. And even though she has a diploma, she does not feel she learned very much. As she has told Mira, "They were just trying to move students on and some of the students they move on never learned the material they needed to learn." That's something her mother wanted to ensure did not happen to Mira.

In fact, one reason that many parents don't realize how bad their neighborhood schools are is that their kids are getting decent grades— they're just passed along. The parents assume that the kids must be learning something, but it is only when the kids try college or getting a job that they realize something has been missing all along. Some parents, says James Coleman, just can't focus on the problems with education. "If you tell a mother that there is a 52 percent graduation rate in the Denver public schools, what does that mean? What does that mean to a single mom who has two or three jobs and multiple kids and is struggling? She's just trying to make it. She's not trying to thrive. She's trying to survive."

In recent years, Mira's mother has returned to school to train as a dental hygienist, but working full time while trying to raise five children means that her own education has not been a priority. Mira's father did not even finish middle school.

When Mira completed Annunciation, she applied to Arrupe Jesuit High School. A member of the Cristo Rey network of Catholic schools, Arrupe requires students to work in an office one day a week in order to help pay for their tuition. The remainder of Mira's high school tuition was covered by ACE. Arrupe offered Mira the kind of education and vocational experiences that her neighborhood public school simply could not. It taught her to value learning for its own sake but also showed her a way out of her situation.

An Innovative New Model

The high school Mira attended, Arrupe Jesuit High School, is part of the innovative Cristo Rey network. Twenty-six Cristo Rey high schools across the country share the same model: students follow a rigorous college-prep curriculum but spend at least one day every week developing skills and gaining valuable work experience at law firms, banks, and a variety of other companies. Each student is part of a team that shares a full-time job which funds the majority of their tuition. Students receive special training in basic office skills in a summer session before they begin work. A significant number of CSF scholarship alumni have attended Cristo Rey schools.

Source:
http://www.cristoreynetwork.org/

Arrupe was relentless about academic excellence, Mira recalls. Her teachers understood Mira's life at home. They realized she was under extreme time constraints. Her mother worked nights so Mira had to take care of the kids, but she also had hours of homework. "They still forced me to do all the homework that everybody else did, which was hard. But I made it. I'm here now."

This is a story that you hear again and again when you talk to kids who go from inner-city schools with little concern for individual students to smaller private or charter schools. The teachers take the time to understand what is going on at home but it does not serve as an excuse. Another boy in the ACE program failed to do his homework a few days in a row and was put in detention. Not turning in assignments was definitely out of character for him, his teachers noticed, and so the principal decided to investigate. He found that the family's electricity had been cut off.

It would have been easy for Mira's teachers at Arrupe to let her off the hook. Look, they could have said, there's no way she's going to be able to hack it here with all of the additional burdens she has on her shoulders. But what good would that have done for her in the long run? As Mira says, "If I had gone to my local public school, I probably would be pregnant by now." She doubts she would have graduated. And like a number of her friends from the neighborhood, she might even have been pressured to join a gang.

There is an enormous need in the poorer sections of Denver for an alternative to the public schools. But unfortunately, many of the Catholic schools are actually closing down for lack of students. Carlos Hernandez says that partly the problem is information. Parents don't know that aid is available. ACE has started to advertise on Spanish language television and has asked local priests to please emphasize when they talk about Catholic schools that families—even those where parents are employed and making a small salary—can seek help. It can make all the difference in the trajectories of these children's lives.

When Mira was a senior in high school, she remembers being asked to write a twelve-page research paper. "Are you kidding?" she and her classmates joked with the teacher, Ms. Carson. "We're not even in college yet. Why are you giving this to us?" Ms. Carson, though, told the students she wanted to make sure they had the experience before they graduated. And sure enough, Mira says she was "overprepared" when she started college. Now, as a sophomore, she thinks to herself, "Okay, this is all we have for homework?" Community college has seemed like a "breather."

Many of Mira's friends from her neighborhood did not graduate high school and the ones who have made it to community college are not really ready for college-level work. In her community, Mira says, "sometimes you are forced into doing other things like work and trying to support your family." The fact that Mira didn't have to make that choice, that her teachers understood where she was coming from but told her she could and should go to college anyway, was very important.

Mira plans to transfer to Colorado University at Denver at the end of her sophomore year. She wanted to save money on the first two years of classes by attending a community college. And then she envisions finishing her nursing degree and possibly even attending medical school.

Other recipients of ACE scholarships describe how their high school teachers and counselors really took the time to find out where their students' passions lie and even introduce them to entirely new fields of study and career options. Linda Chavez was the first student in her family to go to college. "This was completely new to me," she said. "I had absolutely no idea what to do. The school guided me every step of the way." The teachers noticed she was strong in math and science and asked her if she had ever thought about engineering. Linda attended a number of weekend programs to see what an engineering course of study would be like. She ended up getting a full scholarship to the Colorado School of Mines.

The academic rigor that Mira found at Annunciation was not the only thing that put her in the position she is in today. The opportunity to work in different professional environments gave Mira a sense of what careers were open to her. In ninth grade, she worked at a local hospital in the HR department, making information packets for employees, answering phones, and doing other clerical work. She spent the next two years at a local law firm where she was offered more responsibilities. In addition to the faxing, filing, and copying, she helped put together PowerPoint presentations. And she spent her senior year at a large insurance company putting information into their computers.

Though she eventually decided that she could not envision herself sitting behind a desk in her career, she found these experiences tremendously helpful for her development. "I didn't know how to communicate," she says. She was nervous around adults. But after four years in these offices, she has no problem in professional settings. In school, too, her teachers forced her to participate in class discussions. It wasn't simply enough to do the work. She had to present her thoughts articulately in front of other students and adults.

Of course Arrupe, like all the Cristo Rey schools, ensures that the students meet certain high standards in terms of their appearance and their conduct in an office environment. Mira says that in school and in the offices, she was not allowed to chew gum. She had to respect her teachers and her bosses. Her clothes had to be ironed and modest.

The hard work she put in at these offices paid off for Mira in other ways as well. "I got plenty of advice," Mira laughs. She found mentors in each office to give her suggestions about her education and her career. Some of it was just practical. "Don't use slang," she remembers being told.

Many of them just wanted her to know that their doors were always open. A mentor at the law firm where she worked was good at math and said, "When you're in college or even when you're in high school, if you ever need help, let me know."

So far, Mira has not needed to take her up on the offer, but she has stayed in touch and is comforted to know that there are several adults in her life to whom she can turn for personal or professional advice.

Other Arrupe graduates also describe the enormous generosity they encountered in their office environments. Faviana Oropeza, who is going to community college in Denver and planning to transfer to CU, says that for a fourteen-year-old it can be "especially intimidating to walk into a law firm full of adults," but now she realizes, "I'm ready for any kind of tasks that somebody might ask of me. And I'll try to do my best. If I have questions, I'll ask." She notes that "so many of the people I worked with have wisdom that they wanted to share." When she worked at a dentist's office, she found that a few of the doctors would "come and talk to me during lunch. They asked me what I was planning for my future and told me not to worry about certain things but to really focus on others."

Mira's time at Arrupe involved more than schoolwork and her office job. She played volleyball and ran track. She volunteered at a senior center, where she and some of her classmates would bake cookies, play games, and just talk to the residents. Mira found it fulfilling. "If they didn't have us they would be sitting there for the entire day doing nothing." She loved learning about their lives when they were younger.

When we talk about overscheduled teenagers, we usually mean middle- and upper-class kids whose parents pack in activities to build up a college resume. This was not Mira. She hardly understood the college game when she started high school. She seems to have found joy in everything she pursued. But it's hard to imagine how she fit everything into her schedule—her job, sports, volunteering, her schoolwork, and taking care of her younger siblings.

Mira says that "Arrupe's goal was to keep us busy, to keep us focused. I really enjoyed that we were pushed." Arrupe's interest in Mira has remained long after graduation. Not only does she work at the school three days a week as a receptionist, but she continues to see and seek the advice of teachers and her college counselor who is helping plot her move to a four year university.

Her former teachers are always inquiring about how school is going, asking about her younger siblings and offering their help. Her former science teacher has offered help with her biology classes if she needs it.

She has not so far, but she knows that these classes will become harder. She enjoys the experiments they perform and she can't wait to put this all to use in her career. But for now even putting on a lab coat gets her excited about the future.

Mira liked the fact that Arrupe students attended Mass together once a month. "It was a time," she says, "to reflect and thank God that we're here and think about all He has done for us." She recalls the time, which also included the opportunity for confession, as an opportunity to "take a moment and think about our lives and where we're headed."

A few days before I met Mira she had attended a Magis Night at Arrupe. Regular fund-raising events at the school, these evenings put Mira and her fellow students and alumni into contact with professionals from a variety of backgrounds. They are there to show just how vital an Arrupe education can be.

At these events, Mira is reminded of how her life has been completely turned around by the people who support the CSF affiliated ACE Scholarship program. "I remember when I was little," she tells me, "I learned you had to make things happen on your own and you can't ask for help because everybody is looking out for themselves." She had this feeling that everyone in the world was "selfish." But her time at Annunciation and Arrupe completely changed her outlook on the world.

"Wow, there are people who want to help you and people who want you to be better and go to college," she gradually realized. "Wow! Are you kidding me? All these people want to help?"

Though donors have been extraordinarily generous, there is, every year, an unmet need for more scholarships. The organization has tried to get community support for a public voucher program in the Denver area. Both Hernandez and Coleman are out making their pitch to black and Hispanic leaders to drum up support for it. But they worry that the politics are not working in their favor. Privately many of the local politicians and community activists voice their support for giving poor kids access to private schools, but out in the open they don't want to take any controversial positions.

Coleman has started taking the issue back to the ACE families. "What if we closed down?" he asks them. "You're getting two or three thousand dollars a year from us. What's your Plan B?" Coleman says he asked two parents those questions just the other day and they had no answer. Coleman doesn't want to sound coldhearted, but he wants parents who have benefited from the program to think about how important it is to them. And he wants them to go spread the word to other people in the community. There is a need to build a critical mass of support, for people to tell their community leaders and their elected representatives that this program and others like it around the country can mean the difference between a child who goes to college and one who ends up on the streets. The expansion of scholarships could mean that whole communities would have the chance to move up the economic ladder.

Like many recipients of these scholarship programs, Mira spends some time every few months writing thank you notes to the donors. She is amazed at the number of people who give to ACE. She says she wishes she could do more to support the program, but it probably won't be possible until she finishes school. For now, writing these letters gives her a great feeling. "It's that 'Oh wow' moment. It feels good that I'm not alone like I thought I was."

9

FOOD FOR THE SPIRIT AND THE MIND

Danielle Stone at her graduation from Archbishop Curley Notre Dame High School in Miami. *Courtesy of the Stone family.*

In 1998, when Children's Scholarship Fund was founded, John Kirtley, the founder of a private equity firm in Tampa, joined forces with the national organization to launch Children's Scholarship Fund of Tampa Bay. He raised money for 750 underprivileged children to attend private schools and received matching funds from CSF. But the funds ran out quickly. Within a year, CSF Tampa Bay had received over 12,500 applications. And that was with almost no advertising. Clearly, the demand was outpacing the supply.

Quickly, Kirtley and his colleagues began working on legislation that would allow lower-income children to use vouchers and tax credit scholarships to get the education they deserved. By 2001, school choice had been signed into law by Florida governor Jeb Bush. Lawmakers established the McKay Scholarships, private school funding for children with special needs, and corporate tax credit scholarships for kids from low-income families.[1]

Doug Tuthill, who is the president of Step Up For Students, the successor to CSF Tampa Bay, which now administers the corporate tax credit scholarships, says it was important for the program to *start* out privately funded. "We already had a constituency for the scholarship. These families could go to the legislators and put a face on the concept."

Often, Tuthill says, "you get into political fights and legislators like to pretend that this doesn't have anything to do with parents." But CSF Tampa Bay encouraged parents to tell their story. "When parents sit around the kitchen table trying to decide how to best meet their children's needs, that's not a political discussion. That's a pragmatic discussion about how to help a child."

There were more than sixty thousand children in Florida receiving tax credit scholarships for private schools in the fall of 2013. The average income for a family who receives one of these scholarships is $24,000 a year. Families contribute approximately $1,000 per child in tuition. Corporate tax credits fund the $286 million needed to provide the scholarships. Corporations, says Tuthill, often prefer to contribute to this fund rather than just pay to the general state coffers. Their owners "believe in equal opportunity. They want to level the playing field. It makes them feel good as corporate citizens to help the most disadvantaged kids have a more equal shot at being successful."

Every year, the amount of the credits can grow by 25 percent without intervention from the state legislature, assuming 90 percent of the program slots are filled. In order to meet demand, though, Tuthill and his colleagues plan to ask for an even larger increase next year.

Tax credits in Florida are not really controversial anymore. There is not a big political fight over them every year (or every election). Tuthill doesn't expect any major objections when the legislature is asked to increase the scope of the program. There is widespread recognition in the state that for low-income and special needs children, this is an educational reform that works.

There are about 1,500 schools across the state where students are receiving funding. A variety of religious and nonsectarian private schools participate in the program. Most are concentrated in urban areas—Miami and Tampa being the largest.

By all accounts, the program has been a success. According to a study based on test scores for the 2011–2012 school year, Step Up For Students scholarship recipients, who are universally impoverished and overwhelmingly made up of racial minorities, are keeping pace with the national averages for all students. The implications here are enormous. When it comes to student achievement, these private schools are closing the wealth gap and the race gap.

Behind these statistics are students like Danielle Stone, who graduated in 2012 from Archbishop Curley Notre Dame High School in Miami.

Danielle moved to the Little Haiti neighborhood of Miami shortly before high school. She had wanted to attend a public school with her friends, but one day she and her mother stumbled upon Archbishop Curley when they were out walking. They were both struck initially by how "tight knit" the school seemed. But the fact that it was a college prep school made it even more attractive. Finally, her mother liked the idea of a Catholic school. Though she herself is "Christian but not Catholic," she told Danielle, "You'll be feeding your spirit as well as your brain."

When Danielle's mother asked about affording tuition at Archbishop Curley, she was told about Step Up For Students. She had never heard of it before. The annual tuition at Archbishop Curley was around $11,000. With the public scholarship and financial aid from the school, her parents paid about $2,000 per year.

Step Up For Students

Step Up For Students, which administered Danielle's scholarship, is the brainchild of Florida businessman John Kirtley. In 1998, Kirtley was looking for a way to improve educational options in the Tampa area when he read about the founding of Children's Scholarship Fund. Soon afterwards, he started CSF Tampa Bay, a CSF partner program which received more than twelve thousand applications for its first seven hundred scholarships, convincing Kirtley that philanthropy alone could not meet local demand. He went on to fight for a statewide corporate tax credit program which was enacted into law in 2001. In 2010, legislation greatly expanded the program, which is operated by Step Up For Students and serves more than sixty thousand low-income children throughout Florida.

Danielle is a petite young woman with caramel skin and an athlete's build. She is the daughter of a Puerto Rican mother and an African American father from Philadelphia. We meet on a spring afternoon in the barebones lobby of Archbishop Curley. It is a sweltering day, but the school is using its air-conditioning sparingly. The school building is not particularly elaborate—a kind of flat Florida architecture—and nothing has been updated in quite some time. Across the street from the main entrance are the athletic fields, with a low urban skyline in the distance.

Archbishop Curley had only about one hundred students when it opened in 1950, but as other parish schools closed, it became a regional high school and then it merged with the nearby girls' school. There were probably seven hundred students there at its height; now it has a little over three hundred.

Danielle has taken a year off since graduation to spend time with family. But now she is antsy to start her freshman year at Barry University, a four-year Catholic college in Miami, where she will be a pre-med major. If you had asked her a few years ago where she would be today, preparing for a career as a doctor would not have been on the list.

Danielle was never a bad student. In her public elementary school and the charter school she attended after that, she says, "I caught on quickly to the ideas in class." But "I just didn't care as much for it in my old school. I would listen to the teacher, follow instructions, take the test, but it was all going through the steps . . . I would just do the bare minimum to get by." The only subject she truly enjoyed was art.

By the time Danielle arrived at Archbishop Curley, she needed some tutoring in math but found herself starting at the same point as her fellow students. Slowly, Danielle's attitude about her education started to change. First, she was struck by the extra subjects she was required to take at her new school, like religion and psychology.

Initially she was a little resentful about studying religion. She worried she would be "considered a heathen" because she wasn't Catholic, but they were "very understanding." The school has Jewish students, Muslims, Hindus, and atheists, and the teachers don't push their faith on anyone.

Danielle says that coming to monthly Mass here "opened my mind to knowing God more." And that in turn, she says, "made me want to know people more. It taught me a lot about community." Douglas Romanik, the principal at Archbishop Curley and himself a 1984 graduate of the school, tells me that "the whole curriculum is based in the Gospel," but that they have had people who "even though they didn't embrace Christianity still feel the spiritual aspect through word and deed. Whether it's through behavior or outreach in public service, that's infused through the curriculum."

Sometimes, Romanik says, he worries about whether the spiritual messages of the school are having an impact on the students, but "you have to plant the seeds" which may affect their lives later on. "They come to us as immature teenagers where the world revolves around them and hopefully when they leave they're revolving around the world." They'll be saying, "I have something bigger to do than just worry about my new iPad, the right shoes, the right skirt."

Danielle probably had less of a chance than most teenage girls to worry about such frivolities. Her parents divorced when she was eight. When she was in high school, her mother was diagnosed with ovarian cancer. And while her mother was undergoing treatments, her father was deployed by the army to Afghanistan. While Danielle still had her younger brother and stepfather at home, there were plenty of nights she stayed with her mother in the hospital.

She says that Archbishop Curley provided her with a sense of "stability" during this time. "I knew that okay, I go to school. These are my classes, my schedule. This is what the teachers are going over. My project is due on this date. My sport events are on these days." She appreciated the online system that allowed her to see her homework assignments in advance and turn them in by e-mail if she needed to.

The personal attention that she and her classmates got from teachers made a strong impression on Danielle. When she first got to Archbishop Curley, she focused, like most students, on making friends with her classmates. But over time she realized the importance of building relationships with her teachers as well. They were very accessible.

"Everyone here," she explains, "does more than one job." Her math teacher was a soccer coach, for instance. Seeing them in "more than one role" allowed them to get to know students better. "I like the fact that they speak to you as individuals as well as students." In her previous schools, she says, teachers didn't really talk to the kids outside of class.

Tax Credit Scholarship Programs

Florida's corporate tax credit program, which funded Danielle's scholarships, is the nation's largest tax credit scholarship program, serving more than sixty thousand children statewide in the 2013–2014 school year.

In addition to Florida's program, the following states have corporate and/or individual tax credit scholarship programs: Alabama, Arizona, Georgia, Indiana, Iowa, Louisiana, New Hampshire, Oklahoma, Pennsylvania, Rhode Island, North Carolina, South Carolina, and Virginia. More than 148,000 children attended private schools in 2012–2013 using tax credit scholarships.

Source:
Alliance for School Choice

Her teachers at Archbishop Curley were always aware of the different ways that students learn too. If she went to tutoring after school, she says, the teachers wouldn't just repeat what they had said in class earlier. They would ask, "Which way do you feel would help you understand this material better?" As Danielle notes, everyone has different ways of understanding.

When you ask Danielle about the teachers who have had the greatest impact on her, the first one she mentions is a religion teacher, Dr. Goodall. She calls him "kindhearted" and "wise." At first, she wondered how an older teacher like Dr. Goodall would be able to relate to all these kids. But she clearly appreciated his counsel. "And he made religion fun!"

He assigned C. S. Lewis's book *The Great Divorce*, which Danielle says had a great impact on her. "It explains pride and greed and vanity and how those things affect people." The way that Dr. Goodall explained it to her, she says, "we were able to understand that this really does affect our lives." She and her classmates took a hard look at the way they acted toward each other, toward their families, and toward God.

Alongside her interest in religion and spirituality, Danielle's fascination with science was developing. "I just find it interesting how tiny organisms affect everyday life." When her mother got sick, her exposure to biology grew. "I started to learn about all these diseases that don't have cures and there are so many people who are sick and who need help." Now she aspires to be either a pediatric surgeon or a neurosurgeon.

Barry University was her first choice for college, but it is a private school and the pricetag on her education worried her. So she considered going to a community college first and then transferring after two years. But her mother encouraged her to attend her dream school. Just as Danielle's parents sacrificed to make sure that she could go to Archbishop Curley, they were willing to do whatever they could to help her go to college. In fact, Barry ended up offering Danielle a large scholarship. Out of the $22,000 a year, she will only be responsible for $2,000.

Danielle says of her mother: "Her thing is that you shouldn't just have a job, you should do something you love. You don't want to go to a school that you're not going to appreciate."

When Danielle was in middle school, she remembers counting down the minutes to the end of the school day. But when she started at Archbishop Curley, she says, she was excited to get up in the morning and come to school. Even after she had been at school well into the evening the day before for athletic practices—playing soccer and running cross-country and track. Danielle says that her education on the field was also very important to her development as a student. "At first, I was more isolated. I kept to myself. And then I learned, okay, you're on a team. You have to depend on other people. You have to trust your coach, that they're telling you the right information, that they're giving you what you need to achieve success in the future."

Danielle says that one thing her teachers emphasized was taking notes. She feels confident that she will be able to do college-level work because her teachers have taught her how to read and study independently. They taught her how to ride, but then they "let go of the bicycle."

Preparing students for success is what Archbishop Curley does. Danielle says that her teachers and counselors began talking to her about college when she was a freshman. "They are constantly making you aware of the fact that your GPA is important and letting you know about other things that will look good on college applications." They prepared students to take the SAT and the ACT. Her friends who went to other high schools, she says, thought "Oh wow, it's fun." But Danielle says "time flies" and pretty soon it was time to go to college or get a job. At her school, though, they "show you the final picture early on and they say these are the steps you take to make that happen."

[Danielle] feels confident that she will be able to do college-level work because her teachers have taught her how to read and study independently. They taught her how to ride, but then they "let go of the bicycle."

All of this college preparation has paid off for the school's graduates. In the past five years, Archbishop Curley has had students accepted at Harvard, Boston College, New York University, Yale, Wellesley, Wake Forest, Vanderbilt, Tufts, and a variety of other top schools. In fact, 99 percent of the graduates last year were accepted at four-year universities.

Despite its success, though, Archbishop Curley is struggling the way many Catholic schools around the country are. Romanik is the first lay principal in the school's history and as many of the religious leaders have retired, the school's expenses have gone up significantly. "We have to pay people a living wage to take care of their families and that is much higher than what we have to pay a priest or a nun."

"Step Up For Students has been a godsend for the school," Romanik acknowledges. About 40 students out of the 320 enrolled are receiving a scholarship now. In fact, as the costs of private schools have gone up, many working class students simply wouldn't have been able to afford even the cheapest among them were it not for Step Up. As Doug Tuthill notes, during the 2004–2005 school year, there were 280,000 kids in private schools in Florida not on scholarships. Today there are 196,000 kids not on scholarships. In other words, private school enrollment would have dropped off by more than 80,000 pupils without Step Up. That's 80,000 poor children whose parents would not have been able to choose the best education for them.

For Danielle, things really started coming together her junior year of high school. She says she began to "reflect on everything that was going on, the people I met, the different things I learned." She says she found herself having conversations with her family and friends about the things she had learned and using vocabulary words she had picked up in English class. Even math, which was never her strongest subject, started making more sense to her. And she began to understand how that knowledge was necessary to her future career plans. Even if wasn't always obvious at the time, she says, "you reflect back and see, wow, my teachers really did prepare me for this."

Danielle hopes someday soon she can repay the kindness that she has received through the Step Up program. Even before she can contribute financially to other kids' educations, she wants to "raise awareness" about the program. She wants to emphasize to other parents and kids and policy makers that religious schools like hers are not trying to gain new converts, but rather preparing students for all the challenges ahead. "This is an education to prepare your child for the future, the things they need in life, as well as in a community, a college, a job, and a family."

10

BREAKING THE CYCLE OF STUCKNESS

DC voucher recipient and current Northeastern University student Carlos Battle.
Courtesy of the DC Opportunity Scholarship Program.

Georgetown Day School (GDS), where Carlos Battle went to high school, is about as far as you can get in the DC city limits from the Anacostia neighborhood where he grew up. Children of the wealthiest and most powerful people in the nation's capital are dropped off in luxury cars. The students are dressed very casually and very expensively.

But walking around his alma mater, Carlos seems completely at home. He is smartly dressed too in khakis, a plaid shirt, and a gray sweater. He is now in his junior year of college, but he could easily be a tour guide here, with his childlike face and welcoming smile.

The Georgetown Day campus feels more like college than high school, though students may have even more autonomy here than at many institutions of higher education. Teenagers are congregated in hallways and classrooms, eating lunch where they want since there is no school cafeteria. A few microwaves are scattered through the building. The lockers are not locked. There is no dress code. They address teachers by their first names. Students are free to come and go from campus, though Carlos notices that now they must "swipe in or out" so that the administration is aware of who is in the building in case of emergency. Still, the students choose to spend long hours on campus, engaged in extracurricular activities, doing their homework together or just socializing.

Says Carlos, "You have to be disciplined to stay at GDS and do well . . . no one is going to run and chase you down if you don't go to class. No one is going to wag a finger in your face. You know what you're supposed to do and you should be doing it. It's as simple as that."

Georgetown Day seems designed for students who are self-motivated, and a kid like Carlos who came from a single-parent family in an impoverished, crime-ridden neighborhood wouldn't seem a likely candidate. But the Carlos who is standing here today did not materialize overnight.

He began school at a neighborhood elementary school in total chaos. "There was no order. There was no structure." The fighting was constant, says Carlos. Students were "yelling and cursing and not letting the teacher teach." A student could sit there quietly waiting for a teacher to give a lesson, but not five minutes would go by "before someone is doing something and the teacher has to stop." For Carlos, who has subsequently been diagnosed with ADHD, the problem was even worse. He was entertained by whatever sideshow was going on and he would not be paying attention. "There were so many distractions around me all the time that it was difficult."

His mother, Pamela Battle, remembers "the fighting and the stealing." She even recalls at least one occasion where students "tried to set the school on fire." Her older daughter had graduated from Anacostia High and Pamela says, "When she came out, I thought there had to be a better way." She remembers one of her son's basketball coaches who was homeschooling his nine-year-old son. The boy was doing the same work that Pamela's niece had been assigned in twelfth grade.

Pamela says that the teachers her children had in their neighborhood schools "were not concerned about students. They weren't teaching them anything." One teacher told Carlos's class, "it doesn't matter if I come to work or not because I get paid either way."

Carlos remembers just one teacher who seemed to care about his fate and the fate of his classmates. He remembers how she tried to instill in them the importance of education. He distinctly remembers a show the class put on at the end of the year. And he remembers how "she did not give up on the students, which is, unfortunately, rare in the DC public school system."

But there were "no other options." Carlos says that his mother "understood—she saw something in my brother and me and she wanted to make sure we had a better education than we were getting. She wanted us to go on and do something big with our lives." Carlos's sister is several years older and unfortunately their mother was never able to do anything to get his sister out of Anacostia High School.

When Carlos was in fourth grade he was playing on a basketball team and the coach mentioned to him that there was a lottery starting. The winners would receive a scholarship to a private school. "When my mom heard, she jumped at the chance." In fact, Carlos jokes that it's a good thing he won a spot because she didn't really have a backup plan. The day before the lottery, his mother said to him, "Oh my gosh, if you guys don't get it, I have no idea what school you're going to."

This lottery, which seemed like a kind of magic spell for Carlos's mother—a way for her children to have options when it seemed like there were none—was the DC Opportunity Scholarship Program. Signed into law by George W. Bush in 2004, the scholarships helped offset the cost of private school (up to $7,500 per student per year) for families living near or below the poverty level. Carlos was one of the lucky children to be picked.

DC Opportunity Scholarship Program

The DC Opportunity Scholarship Program was signed into law by President George W. Bush in 2004 as a five-year experiment to fund private school tuition for up to two thousand DC children, including Carlos Battle. The program was first administered by the Washington Scholarship Fund (WSF), which had been awarding privately funded scholarships since 1993. WSF was also where Ted Forstmann and John Walton first met as fellow board members and were inspired to start the national Children's Scholarship Fund. When the DC voucher program was first set to expire, WSF chairman Joseph E. Robert, parent advocate Virginia Walden Ford, Mayor Anthony Williams, and others fought to extend the program, and since then it has survived several attempts at phasing the scholarships out. The DC Opportunity Scholarship Program is now administered by the DC Children and Youth Investment Trust Corporation.

Since 2004, over eleven thousand students have applied to the program. For the 2012–2013 school year, two-thirds of students come from families who receive SNAP and/or TANF benefits (food stamps and/or government welfare). Their average family income was just over $20,000.

But before there was a public voucher program, there were private scholarships. Of these, the Washington Scholarship Fund (WSF) was the biggest. It was where John Walton and Ted Forstmann first met and became inspired to start Children's Scholarship Fund.

Established in 1993 to increase educational opportunities for low-income students, WSF operated two distinct K–12 scholarship programs—the DC Opportunity Scholarship Program from 2004 to 2010, and the Signature Scholarship Program (SSP) from 1993 to 2010. In those years, WSF distributed nearly $63.2 million in privately and publicly funded scholarships, serving more than 6,800 students.

In a 1998 interview with *Philanthropy* magazine, Ted Forstmann said, "I hope this will be the wave of the future—citizens taking responsibility for problems and taking action." He explained his motivation behind funding the scholarships: "There are just so many kids who need a boost that they aren't getting, the way things are now. The point is, there's nothing wrong with the kids. What's wrong is the situation in which they find themselves. We can complain about it, or people of goodwill can step up to the plate and try to do something about it."[1]

Virginia Walden Ford, the founder of DC Parents for School Choice, helped direct parents to programs like the Washington Scholarship Fund in the late 1990s. Her own son had experienced great benefits when a neighbor offered to pay for his attendance at a Catholic school. At thirteen, he had started to get into trouble at school and Ford found that his public school was not responsive.

She had chosen to put him at Archbishop Carroll High School in their neighborhood. She started to see him "flourish in weeks." When she talked to him about why, "he said the people there cared about whether he learned." Ford, the child of two educators and one of the first children chosen to integrate schools in Little Rock, Arkansas, in the 1960s, said she realized "that if you put kids in the right environment they can learn." She says, "even though the statistics and schools had always told me that he was going to be behind," she saw him thrive.

Ford began to talk to parents she knew about her experience. Her organization served as a kind of clearinghouse, helping parents learn about and apply for scholarships themselves. But soon she realized that most of the kids applying were being turned down because there simply wasn't enough funding to go around.

She says that the idea of a public voucher program never left her head. While President Clinton had vetoed a voucher bill, George W. Bush had said on the campaign trail that he favored school choice. So when a bipartisan congressional group came to Ford after Bush's inauguration (and after the Supreme Court declared vouchers constitutional in 2000) to ask if she could find some parents to appear at a press conference to introduce a new voucher program, Ford was ready. She got a hundred parents who had benefited from privately funded scholarships from CSF's predecessor, WSF, to show up right away. For years afterward, Ford estimates, she was on the Hill with parents almost every day, meeting members of Congress to emphasize the importance of such a program.

The army of parents that Ford built, people who demanded support for vouchers from their elected representatives, was mostly the result of word of mouth. Ford says that people would come to her and say, "My nephew got a scholarship; I'd really like to get one for my kid."

Ford recalls, "When I started going into the community, I was told these parents would never fight for their kids," but in the five years of programs Ford worked on, over eight thousand parents applied for their children. It's true, Ford says, that these parents were not themselves educated and they didn't always understand the ins and outs of the system. But she recalls, "I can't tell you the number of parents who said, 'I can barely read myself.'" And that's *why* they wanted to make sure that their kids went to the right school. They wanted to "break the cycle of poverty."

That early work done by Ford and her colleagues, building a real constituency for the scholarship program and ensuring that parents really understood what they had to gain from it, paid off when it came time to transform a private scholarship program into a public one. And Carlos was one of those who benefited from this "scaling up."

He began by attending Assumption Catholic School. "This was the first school I went to," says Carlos, "where all of the teachers had an investment in you and wanted to see you do well and would let you know if they thought you weren't doing well." It was a small school and there were other kids from Carlos's neighborhood who entered Assumption the same year.

He and his classmates didn't have to worry about fighting or any of the other distractions that plagued their public schools. "I could just focus solely on school." And it was a good thing. At his old school, he was sailing through with As and Bs without doing any work. But suddenly, when he got to Assumption, he says, "I had to relearn how to learn."

It is funny that when Carlos is asked about his favorite teachers he immediately mentions a math teacher named Mr. Sheldon and explains, "My mom loved him." It is so clear that Carlos's experience in the scholarship program was shaped by his mother's enthusiasm for and involvement in his education.

Assumption was a strict school and Carlos makes clear that while his teachers were kind and often funny, they would not hesitate to discipline him. "And the principal's office was not a place you'd want to be."

In eighth grade, Carlos began researching private high schools, knowing that he would still be in the scholarship program. He came upon something called the Georgetown Preparatory School, which sounded great—except he didn't really want to be in a boarding program. And so he applied to Georgetown Day. As it turned out, though, the two had no relation to each other. As mistakes go, this one could not have turned out better.

Tuition at Georgetown Day is well over $30,000 a year, far beyond the scholarship amount, but the school covered the difference for Carlos to attend. "When my mother first walked in here, she was ear-to-ear smiling. She said, 'This is the place where you should be and where you deserve to be.'"

Academically, it was a rough transition, though. Even though he had a few years at Assumption, which was head and shoulders more rigorous than his public grade school, he still didn't do well his first year at Georgetown Day. "It was a big wake-up call for me." The teachers knew his background, but they were not willing to cut him any slack on his grades.

"I didn't want a handout," he says, even if they would give him one. "They all pushed me and they understood exactly what my situation was. They realized I came from an impoverished area. They knew I was here for a reason." GDS, says Carlos, made him a "stronger person. They taught me steadfastness." There would be times when Carlos was awake in the middle of the night trying to complete his homework. "Everyone else can go to sleep right now but I have to be up for another hour just doing reading." He would get frustrated, but he knew there were people "who wanted me to succeed—my mother, my brother, my sister. So I didn't want to let them down."

There were so many teachers and administrators who became involved in Carlos's life. He enjoyed English and history and even Spanish (though he says he was in a class way over his head for a while). Math was not his best subject but he raves about his math teachers too. And that is what makes Carlos's experience so significant. He may not have liked every subject and he may not have excelled at all of them, but he understood that's not what school is about. Whatever his own abilities or interests, his GDS teachers made sure he had the tools he needed to succeed later on.

His mother would come visit each of his teachers individually and make sure they contacted her if there were any problems. It would have been easy for Carlos's teachers to simply assume that they could educate Carlos without parental involvement. After all, Carlos's mother does not have a college degree and has no experience with a place like GDS. What does she know about making sure he graduates and goes on to a good school? But just as they do with wealthier families, the teachers at GDS treated Carlos's mother as an equal and understood that were it not for her pushing, her son would not be in this place.

She forced Carlos to come with her for any parent-teacher conferences so he would hear what she told them. To some she would say, "If Carlos gets out of hand you can discipline him yourself."

Carlos assures me that his mom is "very protective of her children. She wouldn't say that to just anybody. She had to really trust the people here, to let me be part of this community." Which was not always easy. Carlos had a long commute—by bus and train. After his sports or other extracurricular activities ended, he often wouldn't be home until 9:00 or 10:00 p.m. and then he would start on his two or three hours of homework, go to bed for a few hours, and start the whole process again at 6:00 a.m.

Carlos threw himself into everything GDS had to offer. He played basketball, ran track, participated in theater, performed ballet. He even started a kind of fan section for the school's athletic teams. There was not much school spirit, he says, when he arrived at the school. People weren't attending the games. Carlos organized buses for kids to cheer on their fellow students at away games and even wore a mascot costume once they got there.

Carlos definitely had a "silly streak," which his teachers enjoyed, but he was a serious student. "They saw where my priorities were so they gave me a little leeway to do things." As a senior, he remembers sliding down a two-story pole in the common area called the "forum." No one came down particularly hard on him but the principal suggested that the freshmen would try this out and hurt themselves, so maybe he should be setting a better example.

Carlos's two closest friends in school, he points out to me in a yearbook sitting outside of the principal's office, were a white boy and a black girl. The three of them appear together in various candid shots throughout. But Carlos appears to have moved easily into different groups—from the athletes to the artists. He was on the staff of the literary magazine and participated in a group that tutored local disadvantaged kids.

All his work and his boundless enthusiasm for all aspects of his school life paid off. Carlos was ultimately offered a full scholarship to attend Northeastern University in Boston. Out of six hundred students who were nominated, Carlos was one of ten to win. His college advisor at Georgetown Day actually accompanied him to the school for his scholarship interview.

When he entered Northeastern as a freshman, Carlos was more than prepared for the experience. "Nothing could be as hard as GDS," he tells me. And he's not the only one who believes that. A Yale student reviewing GDS for a prep-school guide writes, "For upperclassmen, the work load per night can range from about three to eight hours. Most GDS alumni say they are very well prepared for college, often saying they find college much easier than high school. But GDS is not just grueling; it's enjoyably difficult." Because students have a great deal of independence at GDS, they are also prepared for the kind of flexibility in their schedules offered by college. They already know how to use their free time wisely.

Carlos has completed two years of classes and is now doing a semester-long internship at a nonprofit in Boston called uAspire, which helps students in high school figure out how they are going to pay for college. Carlos offers financial aid workshops and gives students information about scholarship applications and ways to save money for college.

Majoring in psychology and social service, Carlos can someday see himself starting a nonprofit to help kids who are in the same situation he was. But until then, he is spending his free time promoting the scholarship program that he benefited from and volunteering in the scholarship's administrative offices.

He wants the kids he grew up with to know "there is so much more out there than just this neighborhood." There is a "mental block," he says "that unfortunately parents and kids and people in the neighborhood have. People in those neighborhoods are just stuck. I just want to break that cycle of stuckness." He has taken up the mantle of Virginia Walden Ford, trying to build an army of families to support the voucher program.

Carlos says that he realizes it is "very difficult for people to break out of their comfort zones." He is "prepared for pushback" from parents and students but he considers it his personal mission to "beat it into you until you realize that what you see around you is nothing and there is way more out there for you than just this."

So did Carlos's mother, who used to host what Carlos calls "Tupperware-style meetings." She would invite other parents to come to their house and help them fill out applications or just find out more about the scholarship program. Carlos said it was a "family effort to change the neighborhood." People are surprised when they find out about Carlos, that he went to a school on the other side of the city, that he graduated, that he went away to college. It causes them to ask him and his family questions about how they did it. "If you can touch one person, it's a job well done," he says.

Voucher Programs

DC's Opportunity Scholarship Program, which allowed Carlos Battle to enroll at Assumption Catholic School and then Georgetown Day School, served almost 1,600 DC children in the 2012–2013 school year. Apart from DC, voucher programs have also been enacted in Colorado, Florida, Georgia, Indiana, Louisiana, Mississippi, Ohio, Oklahoma, Utah, and Wisconsin. These programs served more than ninety-seven thousand students in 2012–2013.

Source:
Alliance for School Choice

Sadly, the program has been repeatedly put on the chopping block by politicians in Washington. Whenever this happens, Carlos says, "I feel like it's a shot directly at me. I've come so far from when I was in sixth grade to now and you're trying to take this all away from us. I don't understand why you would take something away that is legitimately helping."

Over the years, since the scholarship program was first put into place, there have been several studies evaluating its results.[2] But Carlos is able to make his own comparisons. Of those boys who were in that public school show with him more than a decade ago, he says, "many are still in the neighborhood and not doing well for themselves. Some are in jail." If he sees them in the neighborhood, he will hang out for a while. "I care what they're doing with themselves." He firmly believes that "everyone who was in my sixth-grade class had the potential to achieve just as much as I did. . . . That's just the unfortunate truth."

CONCLUSION

In the spring of 2013, Children's Scholarship Fund Philadelphia office received, out of the blue, a check for $10,000. The program's administrators looked at the check and saw it was from one of the families that they had been giving scholarships to since 1999. There were three kids in the family and the folks at CSF Philadelphia thought this couldn't be right. So they looked in their records. Sure enough. The family was fully qualified in terms of financial criteria to receive a scholarship. How could they afford to send such a large sum? A quick Google search solved the mystery. It turned out that the father was a member of what's called the SEPTA 48, the forty-eight transit workers in Philadelphia who had just won the $112 million Pennsylvania Lottery.

The letter accompanying the gift read in part: "We've got the ability to give now rather than receive and we want to give back to this program that has meant so much to our family. Because of what you've done for us, we want to do for others." For these parents, like so many families of CSF scholarship recipients, the money that empowered them to give their children a better education has made them eternally grateful.

The vast majority of poor and working-class families never hit the jackpot. They continue every day to go to work, and try to pay their bills. All the while, these parents are doing everything they can at home—instilling the values they want their children to have, helping them with homework (if they can), keeping out the negative influences of the neighborhood—so that their children can achieve something better. But often it's just not enough. The pull of the world outside is just too powerful.

How can you drown out the influences of drug dealers on the corner or gang members down the block? How can you make sure your child is learning when English is not your first language? Parents are the first educators of their children, but they cannot be the only educators.

When Anthony Samuels describes his mother's reaction upon realizing the CSF was going to allow her to keep her son at the leafy suburban Quaker prep school, he says: "it was like a burden was lifted from her shoulders. She literally felt like she hit the lottery." The joy that parents feel upon realizing that, despite their financial circumstances, despite their race, despite their neighborhood, despite their trouble getting a job, they can give their children something better is incomparable.

The idea of school choice is still a controversial one today. Opponents will say that it takes money away from public schools, that it undermines the cohesiveness created by public schools, that it gives public money to religious institutions. Some who express these concerns are genuine and others merely have a vested interest in preserving the status quo. These are concerns that we should nonetheless take seriously.

As to the first, if we have learned anything from the past forty years of attempting to improve education, it is that money is not the only answer. From 1970 to 2010, federal spending on education has roughly tripled (adjusted for inflation), while reading, math, and science achievement have stagnated or declined.[1]

As Andrew Coulson, director of the Center for Educational Freedom at the Cato Institute, a nonprofit, public policy research organization, testified before the House Committee on Education and the Workforce in 2011:

> we have little to show for the $2 trillion in federal education spending of the past half century. In the face of concerted and unflagging efforts by Congress and the states, public schooling has suffered a massive productivity collapse—it now costs three times as much to provide essentially the same education as we provided in 1970.

He continued:

> Grim as that picture may seem, it fails to capture the full measure of the problem. Because as productivity was falling relentlessly in education, it was rising everywhere else. A pound of grocery store coffee is not merely as affordable as it was in 1970—it hasn't just held its ground—it is cheaper in real dollars. Indeed virtually every product and service has gotten better, or more affordable, or both over the past two generations.

We know that private schools and charter schools spend much less per pupil than neighborhood public schools and regularly achieve better results. And we know that some of the lowest performing school districts in the country spend more per pupil than anyone else.

As of 2011, Newark, New Jersey spent more than $23,000 per student.[2] What could a mother in Newark do if you handed her $23,000 and asked her to buy the best education she could for her son? Well, the annual tuition at nearby Seton Hall Prep, where 99 percent of the 2011 graduates went to college, is less than $15,000. Seniors there were accepted that year at MIT, Duke, Princeton, Harvard, and the U.S. Naval Military Academy. Mom's only question would be what to do with the extra $8,000.

We could have a discussion about whether it's okay to give those tax dollars to a religious school, but this is a question that the Supreme Court has already answered with a resounding yes in *Zelman v. Harris* (2002). And there is little to show that kids going to private schools are having some detrimental effect on their civic mindedness. In fact, it seems that much the opposite has occurred. Private schools have done a good a job at teaching kids how to be tolerant of our diverse society.

Important as it is to deal with these philosophical questions, there is a practical and immediate concern for these children that we as a country cannot put off any longer. As the stories in this book indicate, receiving a CSF scholarship is often the turning point in a child's life—an opportunity that paves the way for many more opportunities.

In a speech earlier this year, Mike McCurry, former press secretary to President Clinton and current CSF board chair, asked an audience of Republicans and Democrats to think about how to move things forward on education reform: "Is there a center in which people come together and wrestle with the differences that they have?"

He explained,

> I don't want to belittle [the differences between the two sides] but
> are they capable of coming together and saying, "We can find com-
> mon ground, we can find places of compromise, we can give a little
> here in order to advance an objective, an agenda, a solution that will
> make a difference for all the good of the American people"? And I
> think that's the question that's unanswered for us now; do we have
> the capacity in our leadership, in both political parties and in all of
> our branches of government, to reach that kind of dynamic in which
> people are working, again, for the common good?

McCurry argued that it was time for liberals and conservatives to put
aside their particular vested interests. "We set that aside because we
say, 'There's an agenda here and it's about our children.' And we've got
to work together to make life better for them and to give them the kinds
of schools, the education and the opportunities that they deserve in a
country that's as great as this one."

So how do we move forward with this new agenda—the agenda that
makes life better for our children?

The first step is to educate ourselves. We must understand the needs
in our own communities. Reading about the students in this book is a
start. But what about the kids in our own cities and towns? Kids who
live just a few miles from us but whose education is nowhere near what
we'd accept for our own children. How are the kids in those schools
performing? Are they being prepared for college? Are they even in a
safe environment?

It is necessary to look at our communities also in the broader context
of the nation. At the end of this chapter, there is a list of books and
websites that will help anyone interested in this topic gain a better grasp
of the history of the problems outlined here and the innovative solutions being offered all over the country.

Looking at the educational landscape can be a depressing prospect.
More than 25 percent of students fail to graduate from high school in
four years; for African American and Hispanic students, this number is
approaching 40 percent.[3] We also know that those school dropouts are
three times more likely to be unemployed and more than twice as likely
to live in poverty as college graduates.[4] Worse, one in ten male high
school dropouts is in jail or juvenile detention. Meanwhile, fewer than 3

percent of high school graduates and fewer than 0.2 percent of college graduates are in jail or juvenile detention.[5] College graduates can expect to earn nearly three times as much as high school dropouts.[6] And finally, cutting the dropout rate in half would yield $45 billion annually in extra tax revenues and cost savings.[7]

Once we understand the need for serious reform, we must start looking at the solutions. Are there other alternatives for these parents? Are there quality charter schools that offer options that might better match a student's needs? Unfortunately, the launch and growth of charter schools is often hampered by artificial caps on the number of charters that can exist in a particular area and other legislation that is aimed specifically at making it more difficult for charters to operate.

Concerned citizens who want to get involved can lobby their legislators and city councilors to ensure that good charters are allowed to flourish and that, when possible, they are given access to the same publicly owned buildings that other public schools are allowed to use.

But what about private schools? How can we ensure that underprivileged children have access to effective private education? There are scholarship programs all around the country that raise millions of dollars and distribute it to children in need. They have rigorous application processes ensuring only the most deserving families receive funds. They partner with schools to identify applicants who might not be able to afford tuition and offer help when they can. Also, by asking parents to contribute something toward tuition, programs like Children's Scholarship Fund can ensure that families have a stake in their children succeeding.

There are few charitable contributions whose effects can be seen as directly as giving a scholarship to one of these children. Some programs combine a scholarship contribution with an opportunity to mentor children. Donors get the chance to know a child and see how much they can grow when they are at a school that is right for them.

If there is no scholarship program serving your area, think about starting one. A few donors can make a huge difference for a few families, for a whole neighborhood. If we want to end the cycle of poverty these families get stuck in, we have to start by pulling out one kid at a time.

These scholarship programs, though, are simply not enough. Every year, sadly, they must turn away thousands of students simply because there are not enough dollars to go around. The most realistic, most effective solution to the educational crisis we are facing is to offer students some kind of publicly funded scholarship program. Empowering working-class and poor parents with only a few thousand dollars (Florida has managed to do this with less than $5,000 per pupil) to choose a school that is best for their children is the smartest way forward.

The results of these programs where they have been tried speak for themselves. Test scores rise, graduation rates rise, college matriculation rates rise. It is not true that every student on every scholarship performs better, but on average they do.

A child who finishes eighth grade in private school is twice as likely to graduate from high school and attend and graduate from college.[8] A study of the DC Opportunity Scholarship Program found that scholarships significantly improved students' chances of graduating from high school (82 percent for OSP students compared to 70 percent for those who applied for OSP but did not receive it).[9] A five-year study of the Milwaukee voucher program showed that vouchers increased the chances of students graduating from high school and going on to college.[10] And the programs save taxpayer dollars at the same time. A 2007 Friedman Foundation study found that school choice programs have saved a total of about $444 million from 1990 to 2006, including a total of $22 million saved in state budgets and $422 million saved in local public school districts.[11]

In 1996, Archbishop John J. O'Connor asked Rudy Crew, then-chancellor of New York City's public schools, to "send the city's most troubled public school students to Catholic schools." Crew and his boss Mayor Rudy Giuliani were happy to take him up on the offer. When the mayor encountered opposition to his plan to take tuition money out of the public budget, several philanthropists stepped forward to foot the bill. They offered three-year scholarships to one thousand low-income students.

Now, almost two decades later, Harvard University's Paul Peterson has compared those kids with a similar group of lottery applicants who differed only in that they were turned down. The results were impressive, particularly for African American students: "Not only were part-time and full-time college enrollment together up 24 percent, but full-time enrollment increased 31 percent and attendance at selective colleges (enrolling students with average SAT scores of 1100 or higher) more than doubled, to 8 percent from 3 percent."

Writing in the *Wall Street Journal*, Peterson and his colleague Matthew Chingos of the Brookings Institution noted: "These impacts are especially striking given the modest costs of the intervention: only $4,200 per pupil over a three-year period. This implies that the government would actually save money if it introduced a similar voucher program, as private school costs are lower than public school costs."[12]

The idea of publicly sponsored vouchers or scholarships is no longer a new one. It has been tried in Milwaukee and Cleveland and Washington and New Orleans and Florida. And while thousands of children have benefited from these experiments, hundreds of thousands more have continued to languish in failing schools as the experts keep trying to solve the problems plaguing these institutions.

But there is plenty of reason for hope. In 1999–2000, there were 349,642 children attending charters and 1,542 charter schools. In 2012–2013, there were 2,278,388 children attending charters and 6,002 charter schools.[13] In 1999–2000, there were 12,052 students participating in four publicly funded choice programs (in Cleveland, Milwaukee, Florida, and Arizona).[14] In 2012–2013, there were nearly 250,000 students participating in thirty-two publicly funded choice programs in sixteen states and the District of Columbia.[15] New choice programs in North Carolina, South Carolina, Alabama, and Wisconsin were passed in 2013.

The time has come to move forward with what we know works and give all children the same opportunities that children of middle-class Americans have. Just imagine families like Carlos's and Julio's, attending schools full of Cathianas and Nyawuors, living in neighborhoods full of Danielles and Aleyshas, working in cities full of Anthonys and Silases, all making up a country full of Jasons and Miras. It all begins with putting the power in the hands of their parents.

When Pamela Battle reflects on how far her son has come, she says attending Georgetown Day School "opened up a lot of doors for Carlos that might not have been opened." She always had high hopes for him—the only question was how she could help him fulfill them. Her philosophy was this: "The role I play in my kid's life is that I don't accept anything but the best." That is the attitude we need to adopt on behalf of all of our children.

NOTES

INTRODUCTION

1. "4th Graders Who Scored below Proficient Reading Level by Race," Kids Count Data Center, accessed October 27, 2013, http://datacenter. kidscount.org/data/tables/5126-4th-graders-who-scored-below-proficient-reading-level-by-race?loc=1&loct=2#detailed/1/any/false/867,38,18,16/107,9,12,168,10,185/11557.

2. Abigail Thernstrom and Stephan Thernstrom, *No Excuses: Closing the Racial Gap in Learning* (New York: Simon & Schuster, 2003), 12.

3. Sam Dillon, "Large Urban-Suburban Gap Seen in Graduation Rates," *New York Times*, April 22, 2009,

4. "Cohorts of 2001 through 2008 (Classes of 2005 through 2012) Graduation Outcomes," New York City Department of Education, citywide data file, accessed on October 27, 2013, http://schools.nyc.gov/Accountability/data/GraduationDropoutReports/default.htm.

5. Paul E. Peterson and Eric Hanushek, "The Vital Link of Education and Prosperity," *Wall Street Journal*, September 11, 2013, accessed on October 27, 2013, http://online.wsj.com/news/articles/SB1000142412788732332490457904267276247260

6. "School Choice Yearbook 2012–13," Alliance for School Choice (Washington, DC: Alliance for School Choice), 11, accessed October 27, 2013, http://s3.amazonaws.com/assets.allianceforschoolchoice.com/admin_assets/uploads/167/School%20Choice%20Yearbook%202012-13.pdf.

7. Ibid.

8. Ibid., 15. In 1999–2000, there were 3,500 students using vouchers in Cleveland, 8,000 children using vouchers in Milwaukee, 52 children using

vouchers in Florida, and 500 children using tax credit scholarships in Arizona. Nina Shokraii Rees, *School Choice: What's Happening in the States, 2000* (Washington, DC: Heritage Foundation, 2000), 5, 129, 181. Florida number from "Voucher Parents Want to Keep Children in Private Schools," *Associated Press*, March 15, 2000.

9. "Facts," American Federation for Children, accessed October 27, 2013, http://www.federationforchildren.org/facts.

10. "Dashboard," National Alliance for Public Charter Schools, accessed October 27, 2013, http://dashboard.publiccharters.org/dashboard/home.

11. "Enrollment in Educational Institutions, by Level and Control of Institution: Selected Years, 1869–70 through Fall 2020," *Digest of Education Statistics, 2011* (Washington, DC: Department of Education, 2011), accessed on October 27, 2013, http://nces.ed.gov/programs/digest/d11/tables/dt11_003. asp?referrer=report; "Enrollment and Staffing," National Catholic Education Association, accessed on October 27, 2013, http://www.ncea.org/data-information/catholic-school-data.

12. Matthew M. Chingos and Paul E. Peterson, "A Generation of School-Voucher Success," *Wall Street Journal*, August 23, 2012, accessed October 27, 2013, http://online.wsj.com/news/articles/SB100008723963904441847 04577585582150808386.

2. A FAMILY FINDS REFUGE

1. Patrick J. Wolf, "Civics Exam," *Education Next* 7, no. 3 (Summer 2007), http://educationnext.org/civics-exam/.

3. CALLED TO DANCE

1. Lucy Cohen Blatter, "East Meets West at Ballet Ball," *Wall Street Journal*, March 13, 2013, http://online.wsj.com/news/articles/SB2000142412 7887323826704578356641642885534.

5. A PLACE OF PEACE AMID A WORLD OF VIOLENCE

1. Earl Shorris, *The Art of Freedom: Teaching the Humanities to the Poor* (New York: W. W. Norton, 2013), 34.

9. FOOD FOR THE SPIRIT AND THE MIND

1. Christopher Levenick, "We Shall Overcome," *Philanthropy* magazine, Spring 2013, accessed on May 15, 2013, http://www.philanthropyroundtable. org/topic/excellence_in_philanthropy/they_shall_overcome.

10. BREAKING THE CYCLE OF STUCKNESS

1. "Great Grants: Washington Scholarship Fund," *Philanthropy* magazine, May/June 1998, accessed on October 28, 2013, http://www.philanthropy roundtable.org/topic/excellence_in_philanthropy/great_grants_washington_ scholarship_fund.

2. For proponents of education reform and specifically school choice, the DC voucher program was the perfect test case. Students who applied for the voucher but (because of random chance draw) did not receive one could be measured against the students who did. According to one federal study of 3,300 students, voucher recipients scored higher on reading than their public school counterparts. Patrick J. Wolf et al., "Evaluation of the DC Opportunity Scholarship Program: Impacts After Three Years," U.S. Department of Education (Washington, DC: U.S. Department of Education, March 2009), Table 3, accessed October 28, 2013, http://ies.ed.gov/ncee/pubs/20094050/pdf/2009 4050.pdf.

In 2010, Patrick Wolf of the University of Arkansas found that voucher recipients had graduation rates of 91 percent, compared with the DC public school average (56 percent) and the graduation rate for students who applied for a DC voucher but didn't win the lottery (70 percent). Source: Patrick J. Wolf et al, "Evaluation of the DC Opportunity Scholarship Program," U.S. Department of Education (Washington, DC: U.S. Department of Education, June 2010), 51, accessed October 27, 2013, http://ies.ed.gov/ncee/pubs/201 04018/pdf/20104018.pdf.

CONCLUSION

1. Andrew Coulson, "The Impact of Federal Involvement in America's Classrooms," Cato Institute, accessed October 27, 2013, http://www.cato.org/ publications/congressional-testimony/impact-federal-involvement-americas- classrooms.

2. "NJ Taxpayers' Guide to Education Spending," State of NJ Department of Education, accessed October 27, 2013, http://www.state.nj.us/cgi-bin/education/csg/13/csg.pl.

3. "As Graduation Rates Rise, Focus Shifts to Dropouts," *Diplomas Count/ Education Week*, June 6, 2013, accessed October 27, 2013, http://www.edweek.org/ew/articles/2013/06/06/34execsum.h32.html?intc=EW-DC13-LNAV.

4. "Education Pays," Current Population Survey, Bureau of Labor Statistics, http://www.bls.gov/emp/ep_chart_001.htm; "America's Youth: Transitions to Adulthood," U.S. Department of Education (Washington, DC: U.S. Department of Education, December, 20, 2011), Table 31a, accessed on October 28, 2013, http://nces.ed.gov/pubs2012/2012026/tables/table_31a.asp.

5. Andrew Sum et al., "The Consequences of Dropping Out of High School," Center for Labor Market Studies (Boston: Center for Labor Market Studies, Northeastern University, October, 2009), Chart 7, accessed October 27, 2013, http://www.americaspromise.org/~/media/files/resources/consequences_of_dropping_out_of_high_school.ashx

6. Neil Shah, "College Grads Earn Nearly Three Times More Than High School Dropouts," *Wall Street Journal*, April 2, 2013, accessed on October 27, 2013, http://blogs.wsj.com/economics/2013/04/02/college-grads-earn-nearly-three-times-more-than-high-school-dropouts/.

7. Henry Levin et al., "The Costs and Benefits of an Excellent Education for All of America's Children" (working paper, Teachers College, Columbia University, New York, January 2007), 59, accessed October 27, 2013, http://cbcse.org/wordpress/wp-content/uploads/2013/10/TECHNICAL_REPORT_v7.pdf.

8. Martha Naomi Alt and Katharin Peter, *Private Schools: A Brief Portrait*, NCES 2002–2013 (Washington, DC: U.S. Department of Education, National Center for Education Statistics, 2002), 24.

9. Patrick J. Wolf et al., "Evaluation of the DC Opportunity Scholarship Program," U.S. Department of Education (Washington, DC: U.S. Department of Education., June, 2010), 51, accessed October 27, 2013, http://ies.ed.gov/ncee/pubs/20104018/pdf/20104018.pdf.

10. Joshua M. Cowen et al., "Student Attainment and the Milwaukee Parental Choice Program: Final Follow-up Analysis," SCDP Milwaukee Evaluation Report 30 (Fayetteville: Department of Education Reform, University of Arkansas, 2012), 6, 11.

11. Susan L. Aud, "Education by the Numbers: The Fiscal Effect of School Choice Programs, 1997–2006," *School Choice Issues In Depth*, April (Indianapolis: Friedman Foundation for Education Choice, 2007), Table 27, 17,

accessed October 27, 2013, http://www.edchoice.org/CMSModules/EdChoice/
FileLibrary/243/voucher_savings_final.pdf.

　　12. Matthew M. Chingos and Paul E. Peterson, "A Generation of School-
Voucher Success," *Wall Street Journal*, August 23, 2012, accessed October 27,
2013, http://online.wsj.com/news/articles/SB10000872396390444184704577585582150808386.

　　13. "Dashboard," National Alliance for Public Charter Schools, accessed
October 27, 2013, http://dashboard.publiccharters.org/dashboard/home.

　　14. In 1999–2000, there were 3,500 students using vouchers in Cleveland,
9,000 children using vouchers in Milwaukee, 52 children using vouchers in
Florida, and 500 children using tax credit scholarships in Arizona. Nina Shokraii Rees, *School Choice: What's Happening in the States, 2000* (Washington,
DC: Heritage Foundation, 2000), 5, 129, 181. Florida number from "Voucher
Parents Want to Keep Children in Private Schools," *Associated Press*, March
15, 2000.

　　15. "School Choice Yearbook 2012–13," Alliance for School Choice (Washington, DC: Alliance for School Choice), 15, accessed October 27, 2013, http://
s3.amazonaws.com/assets.allianceforschoolchoice.com/admin_assets/uploads/
167/School%20Choice%20Yearbook%202012-13.pdf.

RESOURCES

CSF PARTNER PROGRAMS

California

The BASIC Fund
268 Bush Street, #2717
San Francisco, CA 94104
Phone: (415) 986-5650
www.basicfund.org

Colorado

ACE Scholarships
1201 East Colfax Avenue, Suite 302
Denver, CO 80218
Phone: (303) 573-1603
www.acescholarships.org

Seeds of Hope
1300 South Steele Street
Denver, CO 80210
Phone: (303) 715-3127
www.seedsofhopetrust.org

Connecticut

Catholic Academies of Bridgeport
238 Jewett Avenue
Bridgeport, CT 06606
Phone: (203) 416-1375
www.catholicacademiesbridgeport.org

Indiana

Educational CHOICE Charitable Trust
10439 Commerce Drive, Suite 100
Indianapolis, IN 46032
Phone: (317) 951-8781
www.choicetrust.org

Maryland

CSF Baltimore
1000 Saint Paul Street
Baltimore, MD 21202
Phone: (410) 243-2510
www.csfbaltimore.org

Michigan

Children's Scholarship Fund of Detroit
1234 Washington Blvd.
Detroit, MI 48226
Phone: (313) 883-8677

Missouri

Today and Tomorrow Foundation
20 Archbishop May Drive
St. Louis, MO 63119
Phone: (314) 792-7622
www.archstl.org/ttef

Montana

ACE Scholarships
P.O. Box 11707
Bozeman, MT 59719
(303) 573-1603
www.acescholarships.org

Nebraska

CSF of Omaha
1414 Harney Street, Suite 400
Omaha, NE 68102
Phone: (402) 819-4990
www.csfomaha.org

New Jersey

The Scholarship Fund for Inner-City Children
171 Clifton Avenue, 2nd Floor
Newark, NJ 07104
Phone: (973) 497-4279
www.sficnj.org

Catholic Partnership Schools
808 Market Street, 2nd Floor
Camden, NJ 08102
Phone: (856) 338-0966
www.catholicpartnershipschools.org

Tri-County Scholarship Fund
4 Century Drive
Parsippany, NJ 07054
(973) 984-9600
www.tcsfund.org

New York

The BISON Scholarship Fund
P.O. Box 1134
Buffalo, NY 14205
Phone: (716) 854-0869
Toll-Free: (888) 216-8380
www.bisonfund.com

CSF (National headquarters and New York City program)
8 West 38th Street, 9th Floor
New York, NY 10018
Phone: (212) 515-7100
www.scholarshipfund.org

North Carolina

CSF-Charlotte
220 North Tryon St.
Charlotte, NC 28202
Phone: (704) 973-4583
www.csfcharlotte.org

Ohio

CSF Cincinnati
P.O. Box 67
Blue Creek, OH 45616

Parents Advancing Choice in Education (PACE)
40 South Perry Street, Suite 120
Dayton, OH 45402
Phone: (937) 228-7223
www.pacedayton.org

Northwest Ohio Scholarship Fund
5800 Monroe Street, Suite F5
Toledo, OH 43560
Phone: (419) 720-7048
www.nosf.org

Oregon

CSF Portland
Cascade Policy Institute
4850 SW Scholls Ferry Road, Ste. 103
Portland, OR 97225
Phone: (503) 242-0900
www.cascadepolicy.org

Pennsylvania

CSF Philadelphia
P.O. Box 22463
Philadelphia, PA 19110
Phone: (215) 670-8411
www.csfphiladelphia.org

Tennessee

Memphis Opportunity Scholarship Trust (MOST)
850 Ridge Lake Blvd., Suite 220
Memphis, TN 38120
Phone: (901) 842-5327
www.memphisscholarships.org

OTHER PRIVATE SCHOLARSHIP FUNDERS

National

A Better Chance
www.abetterchance.org

Commonweal Foundation
www.cweal.org

Jack Kent Cook Foundation (Young Scholars Program)
www.jkcf.org/scholarships/young-scholars-program/

California

Catholic Education Foundation (Los Angeles)
www.cefdn.org

Guardsmen Scholarship Program (San Francisco Bay Area)
www.guardsmen.org/programs/scholarship-program/

Independent Institute (San Francisco Bay Area)
www.independent.org/students/isf/

SMART (San Francisco Bay Area)
www.thesmartprogram.org

Colorado

Parents Challenge (Colorado Springs)
www.parentschallenge.org

Connecticut

CEO of Connecticut (Hartford, Bridgeport, and New Haven)
www.ceoct.org

Delaware

The Delaware Kids Fund
www.dekidsfund.org

First State Scholarships
www.firststatescholarships.org

District of Columbia

Archdiocese of Washington Tuition Assistance
www.site.adw.org/tuition-assistance

Black Student Fund
www.blackstudentfund.org

Capital Partners in Education
www.cpfe.org

Latino Student Fund
www.latinostudentfund.org

Shepherd Foundation
www.theshepherdfoundation.org

Illinois

Big Shoulders Fund (Chicago)
www.bigshouldersfund.org

Daniel Murphy Scholarship Fund (Chicago)
www.dmsf.org

LINK Unlimited (Chicagoland)
www.linkunlimited.org

Kentucky

School Choice Scholarships
www.schoolchoiceky.com

Maine

Maine Children's Scholarship Fund
www.mccsf.org

Maine Community Foundation
www.mainecf.org/PrivateHSScholars.aspx

Maryland

Abell Scholars Program (Piney Woods School)
www.abell.org/programareas/education.html

Baltimore Educational Scholarship Trust
www.besttrust.org

George and Mary Kremer Foundation (Diocese of Baltimore)
www.kremerfoundation.com

Knott Scholarship Funds (Diocese of Baltimore)
www.knottscholar.org

Partners in Excellence (Baltimore)
www.pieschools.org

Massachusetts

Catholic Schools Foundation (Boston)
www.csfboston.org

Minnesota

Minnesota Independent School Forum
www.misf.org

Missouri

Strong City School Fund (Kansas City)
www.kcsjparishnet.org/CCSF/index.html

New Hampshire

Liberty Scholarship Fund
www.lsfund.org

New Jersey

Student/Partner Alliance
www.studentpartneralliance.org

Wight Foundation
www.wightfoundation.org

New York

Futures in Education
www.futuresineducation.org

Inner-City Scholarship Fund
www.innercitysf.org

Prep for Prep
www.prepforprep.org

Student Sponsor Partners
www.sspnyc.org

Tomorrow's Hope Foundation (Long Island)
www.tomorrowshopefoundation.org

Ohio

Catholic Inner-City Schools Education Fund
www.catholiccincinnati.org/ministries-offices/cise-catholic-inner-city-schools-education-fund/

Pennsylvania

Business Leadership Organized for Catholic Schools (Philadelphia)
www.blocs.org

Extra Mile Education Foundation (Pittsburgh)
www.extramilefdn.org

Rhode Island

Anchor of Hope
www.providencediocese.org/anchor-of-hope/

Texas

Austin CEO Foundation
www.ceoaustin.org

Vermont

Vermont Student Opportunity Scholarship Fund
Call (802) 879-7460 or e-mail vtsos@aol.com

Washington

Fulcrum Foundation (Seattle area)
www.fulcrumfoundation.org

PUBLICLY FUNDED STATE VOUCHER, TAX CREDIT, AND OTHER CHOICE PROGRAMS

Arizona

Information on several private tax credit scholarship programs and
education savings accounts:www.arizonaschoolchoice.com/index.
html

Colorado

Douglas County Choice Scholarship Pilot Program
www.dcsdk12.org/strategicplan/choice/choicescholarships/

District of Columbia

DC Opportunity Scholarship Program
www.dcscholarships.org

Florida

McKay Scholarship Program (for children with disabilities)
www.floridaschoolchoice.org/Information/McKay/

Step Up For Students (Florida's corporate tax credit scholarship
program)
www.stepupforstudents.org

Georgia

Georgia Special Needs Scholarship Program
www.gadoe.org/External-Affairs-and-Policy/Policy/Pages/Special-
Needs-Scholarship-Program.aspx

Georgia Private School Tax Credit Program
www.gadoe.org/External-Affairs-and-Policy/Policy/Documents/
SSO%20List.pdf (list of Student Scholarship Organizations ad-
ministering the tax credit program)

Iowa

Iowa Alliance for Choice in Education
www.iowaace.org

Illinois

Information on tax credit for educational expenses for Illinois residents:
http://tax.illinois.gov/individuals/Credits/educationexpensecredit.
htm

Indiana

School Choice Indiana (information on applying for Indiana's
Choice Scholarship Program, School Scholarship Tax Credit Program)
www.schoolchoiceindiana.com

Tuition Tax Deduction program for Indiana residents:
www.in.gov/dor/reference/files/ib107.pdf

Louisiana

Louisiana Scholarship Program
www.louisianabelieves.com/schools/louisiana-scholarship-program

School Choice Program for Certain Students with Exceptionalities
www.louisianabelieves.com/schools/school-choice-for-students-with-
    disabilities

Louisiana Tuition Donation Rebate Program
www.louisianabelieves.com/schools/tuition-donation-rebate-
    program

Minnesota

Information on tax credit for Minnesota residents who pay for pri-
    vate school or homeschool their children:
www.revenue.state.mn.us/individuals/individ_income/Pages/K-12_
    Education_Subtraction_and_Credit.aspx

Mississippi

Mississippi Dyslexia Therapy Scholarship for Students with Dyslexia
    Program
www.mde.k12.ms.us/curriculum-and-instruction/dyslexia

New Hampshire

Network for Educational Opportunity
http://networkforeducation.org

North Carolina

North Carolina State Education Assistance Authority
www.ncseaa.edu/K-12Grants.htm

Ohio

For information on Ohio's four scholarship programs:
http://education.ohio.gov/Topics/Other-Resources/Scholarships

Oklahoma

Lindsey Nicole Henry Scholarships for Students with Disabilities
http://ok.gov/sde/lindsey-nicole-henry-lnh-scholarship-program-
children-disabilities

Pennsylvania

Reach Foundation (information on organizations offering scholarships through Pennsylvania's educational tax credit program)
www.paschoolchoice.org

Rhode Island

Rhode Island Scholarship Alliance
www.rischolarshipalliance.org/sgos/index.html

Utah

Information on the Carson Smith Special Needs Scholarship Program:
www.schools.utah.gov/sars/Quick-Links/Carson-Smith-Scholarship.
aspx

Virginia

Information on Virginia's Education Improvement Scholarships Tax
Credits Program:
www.doe.virginia.gov/school_finance/scholarships_tax_credits/

Wisconsin

Wisconsin Parental Choice Program (statewide)
http://sms.dpi.wi.gov/wpcp-statewide

Milwaukee Parental Choice Program
http://dpi.wi.gov/sms/choice.html

Racine Parental Choice Program
http://sms.dpi.wi.gov/sms_ppscp_index

MENTORING, COLLEGE PREP, AND ENRICHMENT PROGRAMS

Alumni Revolution
http://alumnirevolution.org

College Summit
www.collegesummit.org

iMentor
www.imentor.org

Posse Foundation
www.possefoundation.org

Prep for Prep
www.prepforprep.org

Student Sponsor Partners
http://sspnyc.org

Teak Fellowship
www.teakfellowship.org

uAspire
www.uaspire.org

SUGGESTED READING

Brill, Steven. *Class Warfare: Inside the Fight to Fix America's Schools*. New York: Simon & Schuster, 2011.

Carter, Samuel Casey. *On Purpose*. Thousand Oaks, CA: Corwin, 2011.

Chavous, Kevin P. *Voices of Determination*. New Brunswick, NJ: Transaction Publishers, 2011.

Christensen, Clayton, Michael B. Horn, and Curtis W. Johnson. *Disrupting Class: How Disruptive Innovation will Change the Way the World Learns*. New York: McGraw-Hill Professional, 2008.

Coulson, Andrew. *Market Education: The Unknown History*. New Brunswick, NJ: Transaction Publishers, 1999.

Greene, Jay P. *Education Myths: What Special Interest Groups Want You to Believe about Our Schools—and Why It Isn't So*. Lanham, MD: Rowman & Littlefield, 2005.

Hanushek, Eric, Paul Peterson, and Ludwig Woessmann. *Endangering Prosperity: A Global View of the American School*. Washington, DC: Brookings Institution, 2013.

Klein, Joel, and Condoleezza Rice. *U.S. Education Reform and National Security*. New York: Council on Foreign Relations, 2012.

Manno, Bruno. "NOT Your Mother's PTA." *Education Next*, Winter 2012.

Matthews, Jay. *Work Hard. Be Nice*. Chapel Hill, NC: Algonquin Books, 2009.

McCloskey, Patrick. *The Street Stops Here*. Berkeley: University of California Press, 2010.

McGuinn, Patrick and Andrew P. Kelly. *Parent Power: Grassroots Activism and K–12 Education Reform*. Washington, DC: American Enterprise Institute, 2012.

Shorris, Earl. *The Art of Freedom: Teaching the Humanities to the Poor*. New York: W. W. Norton, 2013.

Tooley, James. *A Beautiful Tree*. Washington, DC: Cato Institute, 2009.

Tough, Paul. *How Children Succeed. Grit, Curiosity, and the Hidden Power of Character*. New York: Houghton Mifflin Harcourt, 2012.

Tough, Paul. *Whatever It Takes*. New York: Houghton Mifflin, 2008.

Viteritti, Joseph P. *Choosing Equality: School Choice, the Constitution, and Civil Society*. Washington, DC: Brookings Institution Press, 1999.

Williams, Joe. *Cheating Our Kids: How Politics and Greed Ruin Education*. New York: Palgrave Macmillan, 2005.

Wolfe, Alan, ed. *School Choice: The Moral Debate*. Princeton, NJ: Princeton University Press, 2003.

WEBSITES

Alliance for School Choice

www.allianceforschoolchoice.org

American Center for School Choice

www.amcsc.org

American Federation for Children

www.federationforchildren.org

Black Alliance for Educational Options

www.baeo.org

Center for Education Reform

www.edreform.com

Choice Media

http://choicemedia.tv/

Council for American Private Education

www.capenet.org

Democrats for Education Reform

www.dfer.org

Education Next

www.educationnext.org

The Friedman Foundation for Educational Choice

www.edchoice.org

GreatSchools
www.greatschools.org
Hispanic Council for Reform and Educational Options
www.hcreo.com
Home School Legal Defense Association
www.hslda.org
National Alliance for Public Charter Schools
www.publiccharters.org
National School Choice Week
www.schoolchoiceweek.com
Picky Parent
www.pickyparent.com
redefinED blog
www.redefinedonline.org
Waiting for Superman
www.takepart.com/waiting-for-superman/

INDEX

ABOUT THE AUTHOR

Naomi Schaefer Riley is a former *Wall Street Journal* editor and writer whose work focuses on higher education, religion, philanthropy, and culture. She is the author of *God on the Quad: How Religious Colleges and the Missionary Generation Are Changing America* (2005), *The Faculty Lounges . . . and Other Reasons Why You Won't Get the College Education You Pay For* (2011), and *'Til Faith Do Us Part: How Interfaith Marriage Is Transforming America* (2013). Ms. Riley is also the coeditor of *Acculturated* (2010), a book of essays on pop culture and virtue.

Ms. Riley's writings have appeared in the *Wall Street Journal*, the *New York Times*, the *Boston Globe*, the *Los Angeles Times*, and the *Washington Post*, among other publications. She appears regularly on FoxNews and FoxBusiness. She has also been interviewed on *Q&A* with Brian Lamb as well as the *Today Show*.

She graduated magna cum laude from Harvard University in English and government. She lives in the suburbs of New York with her husband, Jason, and their three children.